ROSSETTI'S WOMBAT

ROSSETTI'S WOMBAT

PRE-RAPHAELITES AND AUSTRALIAN ANIMALS IN VICTORIAN LONDON

JOHN SIMONS

Middlesex
University
PRESS

First published in 2008 by Middlesex University Press

Copyright © John Simons

ISBN 978 1 904750 60 4

A CIP catalogue record for this book is available from
The British Library

Design by Helen Taylor

Printed in the UK by Ashford Colour Press

Middlesex University Press
Tel: +44 (0)20 8411 4162
Fax: +44 (0)20 8411 4167

www.mupress.co.uk

Cover image: Dante Gabriel Rossetti, *Rossetti lamenting the death of his wombat* © Trustees of the British Museum

ACKNOWLEDGEMENTS

This is a somewhat whimsical book and I have had great fun writing it. But although it adopts a rather diversionary approach to its topic (there were so many curiosities on the way) it is also a serious book about animals in Victorian society. In writing it I have incurred a number of debts. My friends Tracey Garvey and Dr Margaret Forsyth were ideal readers of early sections and the English Department at Edge Hill University were receptive to a compressed version of the whole thing delivered as a research paper. My doctoral student Anna Maddison has been a source of excellent ideas on Rossetti and kindly made me a copy of the invaluable auction catalogue of the contents of Rossetti's house. I have career-long debts to my friends Professors Chris Baldick and Clive Bloom. I would also like to acknowledge the support of Professor David Chiddick and Dr Frances Mannsåker both for bringing me to the most pleasant city and the most exciting University in England and for sponsoring my inaugural lecture, The Kangaroo: England's National Symbol. I would also like to thank Ms Anna Ward who has been indefatigable in tracking down the permissions for illustrations. Above all I have a debt to my wife Kathryn who was, oddly enough, in Australia when most of this work was done and sustained me through email and especially with photographs of her encounter with Patrick the wombat in Ballarat Wildlife Park. Patrick travels around the park in a wheelbarrow and if anyone doubts the ability of a wombat to put up a fight they need only contemplate the state of his keeper's trousers. When I met Patrick in 2006 he was fast asleep.

John Simons

Lincoln

The Feast of St John the Theologian, 2008

LIST OF ILLUSTRATIONS AND PERMISSIONS

The kind permission of the following individuals and organisations for the use of illustrations is gratefully acknowledged:

Illustrations 1 and 2 Wombats by John Gould, 1863 (Museum of Victoria, Australia)

Illustration 3 Wombat by Thomas Bewick, 1807 (The Natural History Society of Northumbria with special thanks to Mrs June Holmes)

Illustration 4 Probably the oldest stuffed wombat in the world, 1799 (The Natural History Society of Northumbria with special thanks to Mrs June Holmes)

Illustrations 5 and 6 Wombat sketch and engraving by Robert Bewick, 1827 (The Natural History Society of Northumbria with special thanks to Mrs June Holmes)

Illustration 7 The Australian garden at Malmaison, 1807 (State Library of South Australia)

Illustration 8 Marquis Wellesley's wombat, 1798–1805 (The British Library)

Illustration 9 Platypus shooting on the Yarra, 1889

Illustration 10 The Duke of Edinburgh embarking on a kangaroo hunt, Lake Albert, Australia, 1868

Illustration 11 Prince Alfred's Australian menagerie, 1868

Illustration 12 HMS *Galatea* at sea in a storm, 1868

Illustration 13 Obaysch the hippopotamus at London Zoo, c.1852

Illustration 14 Prince Alfred arriving at Government House on the day he was presented with his wombat, 1868 (State Library of Tasmania)

Illustration 15 HMS *Galatea* in Hobart harbour, 1868 (Museum of Victoria, Australia)

Illustration 16 A contemporary map of London Zoo, 1882 (www.victorianlondon.org)

Illustration 17 Rossetti's frontispiece to *Goblin Market*, 1862 (Rossetti Archive)

Illustration 18 Max Beerbohm's version of Rossetti's garden, 1922 (Tate Images)

Illustrations 19, 20 and 21 Exterior and interior views of Rossetti's bungalow at Birchington-on-Sea, c.1878 (Jennie Burgess of the Birchington Heritage Trust)

Illustration 22 Tudor House in the late nineteenth century by T. H. Shepherd, 1850

Illustration 23 Jane Morris in the garden at Cheyne Walk, 1865 (Victoria and Albert Museum)

Illustration 24 Sea lion at Cremorne Gardens, c.1865

Illustration 25 Cremorne Gardens Chinese platform, 1857

Illustration 26 Rossetti in the garden at Cheyne Walk, by Lewis Carroll, 1863 (National Portrait Gallery)

Illustration 27 Rossetti and his family in the garden at Cheyne Walk, by Lewis Carroll, 1863 (National Portrait Gallery)

Illustration 28 A 'Happy Family' (www.cartoonstock.com)

Illustration 29 Henry (Harry) Dunn's watercolour of Rossetti and Watts-Dunton at Cheyne Walk, 1882 (National Portrait Gallery)

Illustration 30 *Rossetti's woodchuck*, William Bell Scott, 1871 (Tate Images)

Illustration 31 Sketch on the reverse of *Study For King Rene's Honeymoon*, Dante Gabriel Rossetti, 1862 (Birmingham Museums & Art Gallery)

Illustration 32 A cargo for Mr Jamrach, 1874

Illustration 33 Jamrach fights a tiger, 1879 (Philip Mernick, East London History Society)

Illustration 34 Jamrach's shop (East London Postcard Company)

Illustration 35 An advertisement for Cross (Mersey Gateway, Liverpool)

Illustration 36 *Sceloglaux albifacies* (Mr Huub Veldhuijzen, University of Amsterdam)

Illustration 37 Baron Rothschild's kangaroo escaping at Euston station, 1903

Illustration 38 *Rossetti lamenting the death of his wombat*, Dante Gabriel Rossetti, 1869 (The British Library)

Illustration 39 *The M's at Ems*, Dante Gabriel Rossetti, c.1869 (British Museum)

Illustration 40 *Portrait of Jane Morris*, Dante Gabriel Rossetti, 1869 (Rossetti Archive)

CONTENTS

INTRODUCTION

This book starts from several perspectives.

It could start, as books of this kind often do:

'If you were strolling down the newly built Embankment in October 1869 you might have been startled by the shriek of a peacock as you passed an imposing Queen Anne house in Cheyne Walk. You might have noticed a stout man in a black cape looking from the upstairs bay window on the first floor, perhaps watching the fireworks from nearby Cremorne Gardens reflected in the blackening Thames – and just as well it is blackening for you don't want to see the real colour of the water and what lurks there although you can probably smell it. And if the phosphorescence had been bright enough you might just have caught the glint of a silver épergne on the table behind him. And if the moon was full too you might just have seen the hint of slow movement and maybe two gleaming and startled eyes peering from behind the silver. The man was the celebrated poet and Pre-Raphaelite painter Dante Gabriel Rossetti. The eyes belonged to his pet wombat Top.'

But it won't start like that – we'll pass over the fact that it has.

It could start by saying that this book started in a moment of great joy when I realised that Rossetti had a pet wombat. I had been ill and was sprawled on a red leather chesterfield reading an improving book. In this case it was Fiona MacCarthy's biography of William Morris – Victorian subjects are always best when you're convalescing. What I was thinking at the time was that I had forgotten how important Morris had been to me when I was sixteen or seventeen years old. I had all his romances in the old Ballantine Adult Fantasy (these were innocent times) paperbacks – still have them actually – they are on the shelves of the room in which I am writing this. In fact,

he was so important to me that I went to university to study Anglo-Saxon and Old Norse, Gothic and Old High German, Welsh and Old Irish with Morris's works as a *vade mecum*. And yet by the time I had graduated with a head full of these languages that Morris loved so much I seemed to have forgotten all about Morris and how inspirational he was to me in those days. 'How did that happen?' That is what I was thinking when I first met Top.

Now, although I had started as a medievalist, my subsequent life had led me in various directions and by the end of the twentieth century I was starting to feel that I had written enough career-oriented stuff and wanted to write something about something I really cared about. So I wrote a book about animal rights and aesthetics. And, as in all of these projects, I managed to gather enough material for another couple of books and was thinking particularly about pet keeping and exotic animals. So when I met Top a whole host of things flooded together. If re-encountering Morris was like eating a Madeleine soaked in lime-flower tea, meeting Top was infinitely headier: the wombat, as Rossetti himself said, was 'A Triumph, A Joy, A Madness'.

So I then wondered if it might be possible to write the biography of a dead animal whose recorded life lasted little more than two months. It would be difficult but it ought to be possible. And, in some ways, the book which actually emerged still has at its core that original project – remember I was thinking all this on my chesterfield and hadn't actually done anything about it at all yet. Could I reach out and try to animate, if only briefly, a little Australian animal who lived what was probably a life of neglect and no small terror, at the centre of one of the most influential artistic groups of the Victorian era? Quite literally at the centre sometimes as from his perch in the épergne on Rossetti's dining table in the first floor front room in Cheyne Walk – you can see it in Harry Dunn's watercolours of the interior of Rossetti's house, unfortunately without the wombat. Top slept through dinner parties (perhaps sometimes observing through one eye) which included

Whistler, Swinburne, Morris, Burne-Jones and, possibly, Ruskin. If Top could have signed his name he would have signed it 'Top, PRB'.

It was no secret that Rossetti had a wombat of course but what I discovered was that there is a good deal more material about Top than seems to have been previously realised or rather no one, except perhaps Angus Trumble, has previously been so addicted to this story and enchanted by the thought of Top as to burrow it out. In the following pages you will not only read about Top's life with Rossetti but also about his life in the shop from which he was carried home by Rossetti's brother William. You'll be given a credible account of his arrival in England complete with the date of his disembarkation in London, the name of the ship he was carried on, and the date he left Australia from Hobart via Sydney. Top was a Tasmanian. He was also very well connected and, from his point of view, mixing with Rossetti and his cronies was certainly a step down in the world. For, as you will see, Top may well have been the companion of one of the highest in the realm.

But I am running ahead of things. The boring brutal fact of the matter was that if I simply wrote Top's life it would not have been the book I wanted you to read. In order to make anything like a proper attempt at it I would have had to go into theories of biography. I would have had to revisit issues around the human/non-human distinction. Asked questions such as 'can an animal be deemed to have a life in the biographical sense?' 'If an animal is strictly speaking a moral patient can it ever be considered to be an actor in anything but a purely instinctual sense? And can this sense be considered a life?' 'Is the writing of a biography of an animal essentially the writing of a work of fiction?' 'Am I not simply exploiting Top and imagining I am making a contribution to serious thinking about animals by writing not his life but the life of his keeper?'

Well, you wouldn't want to read that book would you? And I wouldn't want to write it. But I did want to write about Top.

So let's start again. Rossetti had a pet wombat. But that's not

all. He had the wombat in 1869 and that was an eventful year for all manner of reasons, most of which you will discover later in this book if you don't know them already. What you really have to know now is that this book is not only about a wombat about town. It is also about the part he played in a complex and deeply moving series of relationships. There was the relationship between Rossetti and his dead wife Lizzie Siddal. There was the relationship between Rossetti and Janey Morris the wife of Rossetti's friend and erstwhile patron William Morris. There was William's relationship with Georgiana Burne-Jones the wife of Rossetti's and Morris's friend Edward Burne-Jones. And then there was Edward Burne-Jones's relationship with Maria Zambaco. There were other relationships too and Top lived his life in the centre of this swirling mass. As I contemplated them all it struck me how sad the lives were and how very Victorian in the conventional and clichéd sense of that word. None of the main actors seem ever to have contemplated divorce and yet all were seemingly made for each other – Rossetti should have married Janey, Morris Georgiana and Burne-Jones Maria. They were all fairly young and in old age they would have all been friends. I don't believe that any of them (except probably Burne-Jones and Maria Zambaco) consummated these relationships and none of them seemed to have had any sex with their official partners either. And these were the Bohemians. Top watched all this and, as you will see, was involved as a kind of go-between too.

So the book is also about a particular group of bustling and talented people. People who were inventing the modern world by diving back into the Middle Ages; rich people who discussed socialism while their servants cleaned around them but who were prepared to go to prison for their beliefs; people who accepted knighthoods; people who made chairs and carpets and cups and saucers and sideboards and fabrics and wallpapers and tables and tapestries and books and bindings and poems and paintings and illuminated manuscripts; people who exhumed the dead and played with ouija boards. People who were found dying in the gutter with their throats cut and golden sovereigns in their mouths – people who kept wombats.

It is also about the truly fascinating Rossetti. The more you read about him the more selfish and self-absorbed he seems. If you really had glimpsed him that night looking down from his bay window you might not have been altogether at ease with what you saw. He was constantly playing cruel tricks on the saintly William Morris. He cut his former friend the painter Simeon Solomon after he had been caught cottaging (as far as I can tell Solomon didn't find social ostracism too much of a hardship but, of the entire group, only Burne-Jones seems to have helped him out). He was drug and alcohol addicted. He exploited his sweet-natured brother William unmercifully. He cadged fivers from Ruskin at every opportunity. He frightened his friends with suicide attempts. And to cap it all he kept his neighbours awake with the howling of the animals he kept in his garden. And yet you read his letters and he is a dutiful and loyal son and brother. He was adored by his talented siblings. He had moments of quixotic generosity. He loved children and knew just how to talk to them. He had a swarm of beautiful women around him and was faithful to several. He was, in other words, truly fascinating. And this book will, I hope, give you a glimpse of that fascination as I glimpsed it while pursuing Top down the dingy corridors of Rossetti's famously dark Cheyne Walk house and out into the late autumnal light of Chelsea in October 1869.

There's a lot more too. Who would have guessed that you could go to the East End of London and buy yourself an elephant? There was a considerable trade in exotic animals and it turns out that it was a necessary one as private zoos needed to be kept well stocked. Rossetti had a sizeable menagerie but so did a number of other people and we will meet some of these in passing. And, as you'll see, at least two important moments in Rossetti's life as a painter are closely linked to his apparently unquenchable desire to own what he termed 'beasts'.

There is also the question of the first royal tour to Australia and this leads me to another aspect of this book: the whole topic of Australian animals in Victorian England. Australian animals were difficult things as, like aboriginal languages, they challenged all established thinking about the ways things were and ought to be. It's no fun being a classical philologist and suddenly discovering languages based on totemic relationships not gender and cases and it is certainly no fun to be a zoologist who suddenly comes across an oviparous mammal with a beak and a poison tooth. These were disturbing things. So it's not really possible to understand Top without also knowing something about the ways in which Australia and its astonishing creatures started to infiltrate the English imagination from the late eighteenth century onwards. Top entered a world where people were pre-disposed to be interested in him. Where, although steam ships plied to and fro between Liverpool and Sydney (one with a Pre-Raphaelite Brother on board in fact), the strangeness of the Australian landscape and its flora and fauna were still new. Australia (or rather the Australian states – there was no federal entity as yet) had been a prison but now it was a country where you could go to get rich. It had a rarity value and people were still discovering it – as perhaps they still are. But as you read on you will get some sense of the presentation of Australian animals in literature and art before Rossetti and this will give you some idea of his cultural referents when he suddenly had to have a wombat.

So this book wanders around more than a bit. It goes to Tasmania and to the Oxfordshire countryside. It listens to the clatter of silver forks on fine china at Chelsea dinners and hears the crack of a Fenian gun fired in an assassination attempt (Top was there too: did he flinch when the sound wave hit him or snuffle at the acrid cordite smoke?). It smells the formaldehyde disinfecting a book of poems pulled from a coffin and the droppings of a thousand tropical birds kept in one East End storeroom. It tastes bat's urine and strawberries with the cream carefully removed. It is interested in the significance of names: why is Siddal more exclusive looking than Siddall? How do you name yourself when you become eminent? What do you call an animal you have never seen before? What does it mean when an animal and a person have the same name? No matter how much I stretch out, Top is always out of reach. And

Rossetti and all those fabulous people are now gathered in, like Murray Posh and Lupin Pooter. This book is an elegy.

But don't despair. This book is also centred and focused and the focus is Top. I read about him in many ways: in private letters and private diaries and in those same letters edited for publication – and how different they were – and in memoirs and biographies, newspapers and journal articles. I saw him in sketches and cartoons and tried to imagine him through the iron hull of a steamer photographed at anchor in Hobart harbour nearly one hundred and fifty years ago or through the walls of Rossetti's house. These shifting layers of representations have been sifted and resifted for every last trace of Top and every last trace of the multiple meanings he seems to have held. Top emerges from it all resilient and furry. I hope you will come to love him as much as I have.

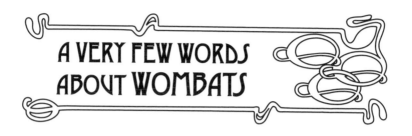

A VERY FEW WORDS ABOUT WOMBATS

WOMBATS ARE, AS YOU KNOW, AUSTRALIAN ANIMALS. BUT THEY are worth lingering over as they are more than just charming fur balls. At least I think they're charming. When an Australian colleague heard that I was writing a book about a wombat his growling comment was 'dirty-arsed little bastards'. But then he probably has had a wombat digging up his lawn. To appreciate fully the story of Top and to understand a little more about how he fits into the world at large it is now necessary to conduct a brief digression into natural history.

There are three main species of wombat. All are part of the family *Vombatidae*. The species are *Vombatus ursinus*, *Lasiorhinus kreftii* and *Lasiorhinus latifrons*. These translate as the common wombat, the northern hairy-nosed wombat and the southern hairy-nosed wombat. The common wombat, as its name suggests, is the most widely distributed. It does have a sub-species *Vombatus ursinus ursinus*. This species is now limited to Flinders Island but it once also inhabited other islands in the Bass Strait so the first wombats known to have been encountered by Europeans may well have been of this now rare group.

The common wombat lives along the coast in a wide band stretching from Queensland through to South Australia and including Tasmania and Flinders Island. It seeks out hilly, forested areas. The southern hairy-nosed wombat, by contrast, is a desert animal found in South and Western Australia. It is more gregarious than the common wombat and has a number of adaptations that enable it to survive the hot dry conditions. The northern hairy-nosed wombat is one of the world's most endangered creatures. A very small population survives in three hundred hectares of Epping Forest in Queensland – not Epping

Illustrations 1 and 2
Wombats by John Gould

Forest in Essex alas. In 1995 there were about 80 individuals which is more than double the number twenty-five years earlier and considerably more, one assumes, than in 1900 when it was considered that the species was extinct. The common wombat has fifteen pairs of ribs while the hairy-nosed varieties have only thirteen. Common wombats have 10–12 caudal vertebrae while the hairy-nosed species have 15–18. So if you ever find a wombat skeleton you'll now be able to tell what sort it comes from.

Male common wombats weigh in at about 30kg although they can be bigger. The northern hairy-nosed variety weighs about the same except the females are bigger than the males; the southern hairy-nosed wombats are, on average, smaller in size but, again, they weigh about the same. They are strong and persistent burrowers and work twisted over onto their backs. They kick the loose soil out behind them and will sometime emerge from their burrow backwards bulldozing the soil as they go. Although most early accounts refer to the wombat as an unintelligent and sluggish animal this is not the case. They can reach a top speed of about twenty-five miles per hour, which is pretty quick – try outrunning a car travelling at that speed – but they can't keep it up for long. They also have, proportionally, very large brains that are fitted into their skulls by dint of deep and complex folds. While the southern hairy-nosed wombat spends its days in warrens of interconnected burrows containing five or ten individuals, the common wombat is more solitary. But they are not completely isolated. In the wild, common wombats tend to live one to a burrow – although they may possess as many as eleven burrows each with strong preferences for three or four – but they do visit each other and, in captivity, they live peaceably in groups. Some of these burrows are constructions of extraordinary size and complexity as was demonstrated by the nocturnal explorations of the intrepid Australian schoolboy Peter Nicholson in the 1960s.

Wombats are mostly nocturnal but, as you will later see from Flinders's account of meeting them, they will come out to feed during the day. This nocturnal habit means that their senses of hearing and smell are considerably more developed than their sense of sight and the fact that their eyes are on the sides of their heads means that their sideways monocular vision is significantly better than their forwards binocular field of view. They are vegetarians living mainly on leaves and grass and because of this their incisors grow throughout their life, which makes them unique amongst marsupials. Occasionally they will eat the roots of trees, especially eucalyptus, and they like to chew stringybark bark and apple box roots to get at the sap. They are very efficient users of water and their faecal pellets are just about the driest of any mammal's. They use dung as a marker and have evolved the capacity to produce more or less cubic faeces: this makes them easier to stack when marking territory. They are not particularly aggressive but they have good offensive armoury and possess not only strong claws (they need these for digging) but also sharp teeth and a powerful bite. If an animal invades a wombat's burrow the wombat will attempt to crush it against the wall using, if possible, the strong bones along its spine – it seems that wombats sit in their snug tunnels much like furry champagne corks and leave themselves hardly any space for manoeuvre although they can turn somersaults to change direction.

Wombats are marsupials but they have a unique feature: their pouches face backwards so that as the animals burrow around the pouches don't get filled with earth. Wombats are usually born in litters of one (although the females have two nipples and twins are not unknown among common wombats) after a gestation of only twenty-one days or thereabouts, and live in the pouch for six to nine months with slight variations between the three species. They stay with their mothers for between a year and fifteen months depending on species, and mature at between two and three years, again depending on species. In the wild they live for five or six years but in captivity they can commonly live into their early twenties. Wombat sperm is marked by its sickle-shaped heads, a feature which wombats share with their relatives the koala bears. Later in this book I will look back at the early wombat tourists to Europe –

frontpackers rather than backpackers – and you will see from these life-expectancy figures how advanced zoo keeping must have been in France compared with England in the same period.

An early belief about wombats, possibly derived from a mis-understood aboriginal tale and perpetuated by the important early naturalist John Gould, was that when a wombat came to a river it crossed it by walking down one bank, across the bed and back up the other side.

Diprotodon opatum was an early species of wombat as large as a hippopotamus. It is now extinct and, ironically, its extinction was probably hastened by the depredations of another wombat ancestor, the fearsome marsupial lion *Thylacoleo carnifex*.

O BRAVE NEW WORLD THAT HAS SUCH WOMBATS IN IT

REPRESENTING AUSTRALIAN MAMMALS

BEFORE WE CAN LOOK AT TOP'S LIFE IN CHELSEA WE REALLY should, as I promised, have a look at the ways in which Great Britain started to learn about Australian animals. This is in order to understand how Top relates to broader cultural and historical patterns and how prepared Great Britain was to welcome him. Not surprisingly it is a story of fits and starts, of confusion and guesswork. How could anyone ever have guessed what lurked on the far side of the great southern ocean? We are now well into the eighteenth century and at the height of the Enlightenment. We have just driven out the travellers' tales of medieval fakers like Sir John Mandeville and set aside Pliny the Elder in the dustless heaven of the classics and unfairly rejected Isidore of Seville as a scholastic booby (his massive *Etymologiae* make him the first encyclopaedist and he is justly now patron saint of the internet). The dear old *Bestiary* and its forerunner the *Physiologus* have been replaced by the new *Encyclopédie* of Diderot and d'Alembert. We know that there are not men whose heads do grow beneath their shoulders – although we have noticed, as Captain Cook discovered, that there really are Anthropophagi. But broadly speaking we feel we have made a good job of ordering Nature. The dragons and sea serpents have been banished to the four corners of the map. We have seen enough elephants to know that they do have knees after all; indeed we rule much of India and ride around on them and how could we get into the howdahs if the elephant couldn't bend down to us? We know that there are no such things as unicorns but that there are such things as narwhals. Everything is going swimmingly. And then comes Australia.

At one level, of course, the discovery of a massive new continent swarming with new and unexpected animals came as a major piece of excitement. There was more out there than people had thought. But when you have just got your taxonomies right you don't necessarily want a whole new set of things to classify especially when they suggest, with the dry wit in which Australians excel, that you got your classes wrong. The discussion below will look at the first encounters with some of the most distinctive Australian mammals (the birds, insects and reptiles are another story) and suggest that a coherent pattern emerges. This pattern consists of encounter and initial description, killing and often eating, preserving and/or capturing live, shipping back to England (or France), full description, published illustration and keeping in a zoo, private or public. What the pattern consistently shows is an encounter with a strangeness that is described in fairly common terms, a striving towards a metaphor or analogy that will enable the Old World public to understand the nature of the new creature and, above all, an enchantment with the curious innocence of the Australian landscape, people, flora and fauna.

The wombat made its first appearance in print to the English reader in Flinders' *Narrative of the Discovery of Australia* in 1798. There is a description and a pretty attractive picture too. And this in itself is interesting as at this time we are beginning to see another consistent pattern by which descriptions, often dry and scientific in tone are being matched against images which are far from scientific diagrams. There is a struggle between different kinds of ways of thinking. The aesthetic and the technical vie with each other in the last throes of the old Roman ideal derived from Horace that one has both to instruct and to delight the reader by mixing the sweet with the useful. And there you have it: the picture is sweet and the text is useful. But the picture is, of course, also useful. Once you have seen it you will always know what a wombat looks like. You might not ever go to Australia and you're unlikely to meet one on your evening constitutional (unless that takes you down the Embankment and past Cheyne Walk of course) but you now have a mental picture and this is the beginning of the country of the mind that is the absolute prerequisite for any empire building. It's not only the people who are brave enough to go there as explorers or miners or capitalists (or unfortunate enough to go there as prisoners) who need to know about Australia; it is also the great British public.

Wombats had first been identified for Europeans by the white convict John Wilson who had been transported for seven years for stealing nine yards of 'velveret' from a shop in Wigan. He had responded to his enforced life in Australia by befriending and learning from the local aboriginal people who named him Bun-bo-e and helped him to scarify his body with traditional markings. Governor Hunter employed Wilson to guide an expedition up river and, on this journey, he pointed out the 'Whom-batt' (as he called it) to Hunter's servant John Price who recorded the creature in his diary entry for 26th January 1798 describing it 'an animal about twenty inches high, round ears and very small eyes; [it] is very fat and has much the appearance of a badger.'

Flinders himself described his first encounter with wombats as follows:

Clark's Island afforded the first specimens of the new animal called wombat. This little bear-like quadruped is known in New South Wales, and is called by the natives womat, wombat, or womback, according to the different dialects – or perhaps to the different rendering of the wood-rangers who brought the information. It does not quit its retreat till dark; but feeds at all times on the uninhabited islands, and was commonly seen foraging among the sea refuse on the shore [like the sheep in A Winter's Tale!] though the coarse grass seemed to be its usual nourishment. It is easily caught when at a distance from its burrow; its flesh resembles lean mutton, and to us was acceptable food.

The confusion about the actual name 'wombat' (in Tasmania the animal was also known variously as publedina and drogerdy; the Wiradjuri, who lived west of the Blue Mountains which were not crossed until 1813, called it guulang and Peter Good, the gardener who sailed with Flinders on the Investigator called it wumot) will become significant in the discussion of kangaroos below, but notice how Flinders is striving to find terms that will be understandable to a European reader in order to describe not only the appearance of the creature but also its taste. The survivors of the wreck of the *Sydney Cove*, which ran ashore on Preservation Island in February 1797, had kept going on a diet of wombats so Flinders knew that the meat was wholesome and had plenty of acquaintances who had sampled it. Interestingly enough, the author of the *History of New South Wales* (1818) reckoned that wombats tasted like pork. Collins's *An Account of the English Colony in New South Wales* (1802) – which also includes an engraving based on Governor Hunter's drawing of the wombat brought back by Flinders and about which he corresponded with Sir Joseph Banks – described the wombat as 'a squat, thick, short-legged, and rather inactive quadruped, with great appearance of stumpy strength, and somewhat bigger than a large turnspit dog'. These dogs, now extinct, were specially bred to turn the spits on which meat was set to roast over kitchen fires; they were chunky and short legged as their role demanded and weighed about 30 pounds when fully grown.

This description was taken from the somewhat fuller notes made by George Bass who was with Flinders on the Furneaux Islands:

> The wombat is about the size of a turnspit dog. It is a squat, thick short-legged, and rather inactive quadruped with an appearance of great stumpy strength. Its figure and movements, if they do not resemble those of the bear, at least remind one of that animal... The head is large and flattish and when looking the animal full in the face, seems independent of the ears, to form nearly an equilateral triangle. The hair on the face lies in regular order, as if combed.

It is hard to imagine a better description for both accuracy and concision and a certain style. And Bass went on to offer a really expansive account of the wombat's anatomy and habits. We will see later how this kind of perception affected Rossetti's view of Top. Bass thought the wombat 'very palatable'.

But the best image of a wombat from this period is the one produced by Ferdinand Augustus Bauer who returned to Australia with Flinders on *The Investigator* and who, between 1801 and 1803, produced a marvellous portfolio of watercolours of Australian plants and animals which, due to a mixture of Bauer's perfectionism and a downturn in the economy as a result of the on-going Napoleonic wars, was not published until the present day. So we are fortunate that the image survives. It is almost certainly based on two dead wombats who were shot by Flinders himself on 23rd April 1802 when he was visiting King Island in the Bass Strait:

> A boat was immediately hoisted out, and I landed with the botanical gentlemen. On stepping out of the boat, I shot one of those little bear-like creatures called Womat; and another was afterwards killed...

The wombats in Bauer's painting look healthy enough. But if ever two wombats found themselves in the wrong place at the wrong time it was those two wombats on that far off St George's day. They should have not quitted their retreat till dark.

A luckier wombat was the one actually captured by Bass in May 1799:

> Seeing one feeding on the seashore and not caring to shoot him I approached unperceived to within thirty yards of the inexperienced creature, then gave chase. When up with him that he might not be hurt, I snatched him off the ground and laid him along my arm like a child. He made no noise, nor any effort to escape, not even a struggle. His countenance was placid and undisturbed and seemed as contented as if I had nursed him from his infancy. I carried him for more than a mile and often shifted him from arm to arm and sometimes, to ease my arms, laid him upon my shoulders. But he took it all in good part. At last being obliged to secure his legs whilst I went into a copse to cut a new species of wood his anger arose with the binding of the twain, he whizzed [Bass had previously identified the wombat's voice as 'a low cry between a hissing and a whizzing'] with all his might, kicked and scratched most furiously and snipped off a piece from the elbow of my jacket with his long grasscutters. Our friendship was at an end; for

although his legs were untied in a few minutes, he still remained implacable and ceased to kick and scratch only when he was exhausted. He was so constantly on the watch to bite that I dare no longer carry him on my shoulder and scarcely upon my arm. For two miles to where the boat was lying, he kept up his pranks.

It must have been a long two miles for both Bass and the wombat. But what a picture it all makes: a young Georgian scientist, presumably in unsuitable clothes, struggling across the scrubby Tasmanian foreshore and a wombat in his arms kicking, biting and whizzing like anything.

The first really popular image of a wombat appeared in the fifth (1807) edition of the engraver Thomas Bewick's *A General History of Quadrupeds*.

Illustration 3
Wombat by Thomas Bewick

This was captioned 'Wombach' and was based (it is a rather attenuated creature) on the specimen which had been sent to Newcastle, together with a platypus (the first platypus had arrived in London the year before on the *Britannia* and may still be in the Natural History Museum), as a gift from Governor Hunter who was an honorary member of that city's Literary and Philosophical Society. The wombat is still to be seen in the Hancock Museum and is recorded as having arrived in the city in 1799.

Illustration 4
Probably the oldest stuffed wombat in the world

As well as being the subject of a cut by Thomas Bewick it was sketched by his brother Robert.

The wombat and platypus arrived in a barrel of brandy which, it is said, promptly burst over the head of the woman who was carrying it on her head after it had been unloaded. Bewick's woodcut was based on a dead specimen of course but another of the Australian mammals in his book, the opossum (first published in the 1790 edition), was based on a live animal owned by the Bishop of Durham's son.

The reports of Bass, Flinders, Hunter and Banks, backed up by the first scientific description of a wombat in George Shaw's *General Zoology* (1800), prepared Britain to host its first wombat visitor. This animal arrived in 1805. Another arrived in Liverpool on 13th October 1810 when *The Investigator*, battered and after many miles of hard sailing, finally came home together with 3,600 other specimens. The creature (who

Illustrations 5 and 6
Wombat sketch and engraving by Robert Bewick

must have had a terrible time on the ship) was given to Eliot Clift of the Royal College of Surgeons for safe-keeping. It was also studied by the scientist Sir Everard Home. Home was not impressed:

> In captivity it is, as a rule, amiable, the amiability being possibly associated with stupidity.

Perhaps Home objected to the fact that 'it burrowed into the ground at every opportunity and covered itself in the earth with surprising quickness'. It is worrying when amiability and stupidity are seen as related but Home's dismissive comments do set a theme that will continue well into the nineteenth century. Wombats are, well, not all that bright. However, as Home only managed to keep the wombat alive for two years we have to doubt that he was really committed to its care. By the 1880s live wombats were still quite rare but dead ones formed part of the trade in luxury goods: you could buy wombat hearth rugs and for the high price of thirty-five shillings (£1.75) you could acquire a wombat fur carriage rug.

But it should still be a matter of national disgrace that the first wombats arrived in France (together with some emus and a kangaroo) on Nicolas Baudin's floating antipodean menagerie the *Geographe* as early as 24th March 1804 (although there seems some doubt as to which ship the wombats actually arrived on – it is possible that one arrived on the *Geographe* and two on the *Casuarina* or the *Naturaliste*, or *vice versa*). What's worse, at least one of three that arrived with Baudin had been given to him by the captain of a British schooner that he had met on his travels in Van Diemen's Land. Six bottles of claret appear to have changed hands. In this year Napoleon crowned himself Emperor and so there was little, if any, opportunity for British naturalists to see these creatures as the wars continued pretty much unabated until 1814 and then started for another hundred days in 1815. In 1802 Sir Joseph Banks had generously taken advantage of the short-lived Peace of Amiens to send Napoleon a pickled platypus but such collaboration would not occur now. Baudin brought back to France some 100,000 specimens (some sources say 200,000) of one sort or another of

which around 2,000 were new to science at that time. This is no mean achievement although Baudin seems somewhat less celebrated in France today than Cook, or even Flinders, is in Britain. When he died on the voyage back to France in 1803 an ungrateful Napoleon – presumably not realising his wombat was on the way – spat out that 'Captain Baudin did well to die; if he had returned I would [have] hanged him'. Baudin cannot have been all that popular with his officers either as when three days out he discovered that his kangaroos were dying he turfed the staff out of their cabins and installed the remaining marsupials. However, unlike Captain Bligh (who will figure later in the story and who disturbed the good order of living arrangements on the *Bounty* by turning over cabins to breadfruit plants), he did not provoke a mutiny.

The French connection is a fascinating one. Baudin's ships bought seventy-two live animals and birds back from their voyage of exploration and a large number of plants and seeds. This mighty hoard was too good all to go to the national collection in the Jardin des Plantes and was divided between that institution and Napoleon himself – or rather Joséphine, whose imagination was caught by these exotic strangers. So off to Malmaison they went, together with an artist who painted an emu on the ceiling of Joséphine's boudoir. The most famous flower-painter of the age, Redouté, was commissioned to illustrate a book on the Malmaison garden which became the first major work on Australian flora to be published anywhere. Baudin's own artists, Charles Lesueur and Nicholas-Martin Petit, also produced a lavish book, *Voyages de Découvertes aux Terres Australes*, which includes a wonderful illustration of a wombat. But best of all is the vignette on the title page. This shows the house of Malmaison itself and its gardens.

The gardens are full of Australian plants and on the lawn are a kangaroo, a dwarf emu and a black swan. I look in vain for the wombat but my guess is that it has burrowed into the turf. It is pleasant to speculate though that Napoleon's imperial ambition towards Australia might have been stimulated by the desire to have more wombats. Or by jealousy that Marquis Wellesley, the

LA NOUVELLE · HOLLANDE MIEUX CONNUE · VÉGÉTAUX UTILES NATURALISÉS EN FRANCE.

LES CORVETTES LE GÉOGRAPHE, LE NATURALISTE
ET LA GOËLETTE LE CASUARINA.

M·DCCC. — M·DCCCIV.

C. A. Lesueur del

Illustration 7
The Australian garden at Malmaison

Duke of Wellington's brother, and one of Flinders's powerful friends had a pet wombat of his own. This can be seen in a very nice watercolour now in the British Museum.

Given the likely dates that the picture was painted it would appear that the wombat was in Wellesley's possession while he was Governor General of India in which case this wombat was almost certainly the first of his kind and maybe the first Australian to set foot (or paw) on the sub-continent.

The French, largely due to the advanced thinking and enlightened practice of Frederic Cuvier, also made a better fist of wombat keeping than the British. In 1818 one of these

Illustration 8
Marquis Wellesley's wombat

French wombats was the first of its species to be formally diagnosed with sarcoptic mange. It appears that not all three had the disease which does suggest they were kept on separate ships on the voyage back and, subsequently, were kept apart so that the mites that cause the condition did not travel from one animal to another. But notice the date. This wombat, mange and all, had lived in France for fourteen years – that is pretty good going. (It is not, however, as good as that achieved by Cardinal Wolsey's pet tortoise who appears to have survived for three hundred and fifty years in the grounds of Hampton Court until it came second in a bout with a motor mower; or – come to that – military tortoises such as Timmy who was with the British army at the siege of Sebastopol and died as recently as 2003 or Ali Pasha who was captured while serving with the Turks at Gallipoli and is still under house arrest in Lowestoft.) The wombats in the Jardin des Plantes during the siege of Paris in 1870 did not, however, fare so well. They were sold off at what *The Times* described somewhat sniffily as 'a fancy price' and put in a ragoût.

Slowness and torpor were not associated only with wombats but was also seen as a distinguishing characteristic of the koala bear, another of Australia's astonishing animals. In his *Arcana; or the Museum of Natural History* (1811) George Perry offers both the first picture of a koala and a rather unflattering description of the animal he calls Koalo or New Holland Sloth:

> Amongst the numerous and curious tribes of animals, which the hitherto almost undiscovered regions of New Holland have opened to our view, the creatures we are now about to describe stands singularly pre-eminent. Whether we consider the uncouth and remarkable form of its body, which is particularly awkward and unwieldy, or its strange physiognomy and manner of living, we are at a loss to imagine for what particular scale of usefulness or happiness such an animal could by the great Author of Nature possibly be destined. As Nature however provides nothing in vain, we may suppose that even those torpid, senseless creatures are wisely intended to fill up one of the great links of the chain of animated nature.

Again, the newly discovered animal is seen as somehow insufficient. It is as if its long exile away from the vitalising influence of European culture has made it, like the wombat, stupid and slow. And Perry's anxiety about the place of the koala in nature – we wouldn't now look at an animal and ask 'what is it for?' – sums up the mindset of the pre-Darwinian zoologist and shows, most eloquently, why the animals of the newly discovered southern islands created such a problem and such an opportunity.

The koala bear (but, of course, it isn't a bear: nothing in Australian zoology is ever anything like it seems) was first spotted by John Price, a servant of the New South Wales governor John Hunter, on 26th January 1798 – this was on the expedition with Wilson where the 'whom-batt' was also first sighted. He reported back as follows:

> There is another animal which the natives call a cullawine, which much resembles the sloths in America.

A certain Ensign Barralier managed to get two koala feet (the head it seems had disappeared) in exchange for 'two spears and a tomahawk' and sent them to Governor King in a bottle of brandy. In 1803 he finally got hold of a live specimen (an adult with two babies) which the *Sydney Gazette* described at some length concluding that:

> The surviving Pup generally clings to the back of the mother, or is caressed by her with a serenity that appears peculiarly characteristic; it has a false belly like the apposim [sic], its food consists exclusively of gum leaves in the choice of which it is excessively nice. It was known as a Colo.

Sir Everard Home however called it the koala and this name has stuck although Home's belief that it was a species of wombat has not – although wombats and koala bears are, in fact, related. *Koala* appears to be an aboriginal word but if one considers the wealth of names which were used by the early colonists and which, presumably, mainly derive from attempts to transliterate a host of various words in local languages it is easy to see that this may not actually be the case. Early names include Culawine, Karbor, Colo, Koolah, Colah, Koolewong, Boorabee, Burroor, Bangaroo (I like that one; what a pity it didn't catch on), Banjorah, Burrenbong, Pucawan and Goribun. This astonishing variation probably covers a word not for the koala but for a local aboriginal people. When the first live koolah was brought to Sydney what became an icon of Australian wildlife (and the QANTAS airline) had, by virtue of its new – almost Latinate – name, already become part of the new colonial world.

The echidna or spiny anteater is another distinctively Australian animal. This is quite a rarity being, together with the platypus, the other member of the mammalian order *monotreme*. It appears that the first European to encounter an echidna was none other than Captain Bligh of the *Bounty*. In 1790, while on his epic voyage in the open boat, he and his crew pulled into Tasmania. Here they encountered an echidna and what else was there to do but kill it and eat it? But before it went into the pot (it had a 'delicate flavour' – but you must remember these men had spent a fairly long time in an open boat by this time) this echidna was the subject of a surprisingly skilful and meticulous drawing made by Bligh himself – who commented, alarmingly, that the echidna's mouth would not open wide enough to introduce the muzzle of a pistol – and finally published in 1802 by Sir Everard Home. In 1792 George Shaw first described the echidna using a pickled example that had been sent from Australia on *HMS Gorgon*. Shaw mistakenly assumed, because of its snout and, presumably, the fact that it was reported captured on an anthill, that it was an anteater (by now you won't be surprised to learn that it isn't). When Home had a go at classifying the animal ten years later he used Shaw's specimen and Bligh's drawing and determined that it was a mammal. It was not until 1884 that it was realised that echidnas lay eggs. Bligh eventually returned to Australia as Governor of New South Wales in 1806. By 1808 the garrison had mutinied. Bligh was imprisoned and in 1810 returned to England to plead his case. Bligh was exonerated as he was in the case of the *Bounty* incident. He ended his life as an admiral. But what an extraordinary career: two mutinies and the first European sighting (and eating) of an echidna.

An important thing that needs to be said about all this at this point and a thing that, I think, helps to contextualise a good deal of the emergent way of thinking around Australian animals is that Australia offers a very rare case of colonisation by settlement rather than conquest. Now, I am not suggesting here that there was not a good deal of violence and, arguably, actual genocide in some areas. What I am saying is that when they got to Australia British colonists did not have to face well-organised Zulu impis disciplined by tradition and *esprit de corps*, Maori infantry regiments whose tactical evolutions were more than a match for British military science, or huge Mughal hordes bristling with all manner of elephant-mounted cannon, camels carrying jezails, and French advisers. Australia just let the colonists in. It was difficult after a bit to understand that the great continent was populated at all as the indigenous people's social organisation was so alien. This led to application of the doctrine of *terra nullius* by which the Crown could claim the continent without any reference to any potential pre-existing property rights.

Often when the British started to take an interest in another country they sought to understand local societies in terms of their own categories. So the early settlers of the east coast of North America dealt with what they considered to be local kings and were always on the look out for a kind of super king with whom they could do real business. India was easy, only the most obtuse and closed-minded Englishman could fail to see the evidence of sophisticated civilisation around him and China was much the same, albeit in sad decline. Africa was a bit more of a challenge but, although disturbed by their perceptions that they were dealing with very primitive people, the imperialists nonetheless soon got on with working out who was in charge and treating him (or her) as a monarch. Later on they discovered that the oral histories on which they based their decisions, in East Africa at least, actually changed to fit the current situation and to provide whoever happened to be in charge at the time with a suitable lineage.

None of this was so easy with Australia where you had highly dispersed and shifting populations, massively diversified languages and no sign of any buildings except a few basic huts. That must have been the really scary thing. There was nothing there. James Cook expressed some very typical Enlightenment sentiments when he described the Australian peoples:

> From what I have said of the natives of New Holland they may appear to some to be the most wretched people upon earth; but in reality they are far happier than we Europeans, being wholly unacquainted not only with the superfluous, but with the necessary conveniences so sought after in Europe; they are happy in not knowing the use of them. They live in a tranquillity which is not disturbed by the inequality of condition.

Just as the animals are torpid and 'inexperienced' so the local people live in a mean but happy state. This is, of course, an enormously attractive state of affairs to Europeans who were filled with the ideas later to be associated with Rousseau and Wordsworth and who wanted desperately to see an uncorrupted state of nature. It is also a pushover for colonists. All this may seem an unnecessary digression, however brief, but the nature of Australia and its settlement had very great significance for the fate of the wildlife and the ways in which it was understood in the old country. And for the way Rossetti took to Top.

Wombats were rarities until the 1850s – more of that below – but another Australian mammal was somewhat better known and deserves more extensive treatment. That was, of course, the kangaroo and the kangaroo provides a particularly instructive example of the introduction of an entirely alien creature into the British imagination. In addition, unlike the wombat or koala, the kangaroo was clearly no slouch although as we shall see its actual name caused plenty of uncertainty and doubt.

The creature's name turns out to have a very strange history. The word 'kangaroo' first appears in Captain Cook's journals of 1770 and had been collected from the aboriginal Guugu Yimidhirr people who used it to describe large black kangaroos. Not just any kangaroos note: large black kangaroos. This very specific meaning was subsequently and probably not surprisingly the cause of rich confusion. It was also, from the point of view of clarifying what word went with what animal, hard luck as the first encounter between the European Enlightenment and kangaroos appears to have been with a different kind of kangaroo to that first seen by Cook. (Various kinds of kangaroo and wallaby had previously been seen and described by Pelsaert (1629), Volckersen (1658), de Vlamingh (1696) and Dampier (1699).) Joseph Banks's own description clearly suggests this as what he saw was:

> An animal as large as a greyhound, of a mouse colour and very swift.

And, as with Flinders's wombats, the kangaroo soon became the victim of the Enlightenment's predilection for looking at landscape down the barrel of a gun:

> Our second lieutenant who was shooting today had the good fortune to kill the animal that had so long been the subject of our speculations.

Not good fortune for the kangaroo of course who proved 'excellent meat' at dinner the next day. Indeed, John Alexander Gilfillan's painting of *Captain Cook taking possession of the Australian continent on behalf of the British Crown* (1889) actually shows, to the side of the main action, two men nonchalantly skinning a kangaroo while a dog looks on with no small interest. Unfortunately, this painting has gone missing and you can see it only in reproduction now, so if any reader happens to spot it the Royal Society of Victoria would be pleased to hear from you.

When Captain King's party explored the Endeavour River in 1820 they found that although the Guugu Yimidhirr vocabulary they collected was very similar to that attested by Cook the word 'kangaroo' appeared to be missing and had, apparently been replaced by another word 'minnar' or 'meenuah'. There were plenty of kangaroos around but we must assume that, unfortunately for King and his men, there were no large black ones. King's party not unnaturally concluded that Cook's original aboriginal respondent had, on being asked the name of the large black animal, replied 'Kangaroo' which they speculated meant 'I don't know'. 'Minha' is actually a generic term meaning 'an edible animal' which also tells us something about Australia in those days. If you couldn't find a porky or muttony wombat to eat you could always tuck into a kangaroo.

But the confusion got worse and worse. Eighteen years later the Sydney (Botany Bay) penal settlement was founded and the first Governor, Arthur Phillips, came armed not only with a stock of Brown Bess muskets but also, prudently and imaginatively, with a copy of Banks's Australian vocabulary. Governor Phillips was, however, doomed to be sorely disappointed when he attempted to use it to converse with the local inhabitants. When he spoke to his new neighbours they had no idea what he was talking about. This was because they were Dharuk not Guugu Yimidhirr and this distinction was not in any way apparent to the British colonists.

It must have been exceptionally frustrating as, once again, the area was swarming with kangaroos but none of the locals was using the word. To make matters worse, the problem now took a singularly absurd turn when the Dharuk assumed that 'kangaroo' was an English word designating a generic group of animals. They then asked if cows were kangaroos. Phillips must have stumped home in high dudgeon and presumably followed by a sniggering squad of Royal Marines. He had come all this way, made all this effort and look what happens: they think that cows are kangaroos. It wasn't even as if, in all this heat, he could have had the satisfaction of throwing Banks's book on the fire. He must have flopped down in his makeshift home with the wig powder clumping in the sweat on his neck and his leather stock chafing his throat as never before.

By the 1820s, when British settlers had started to colonise the banks of the Darling, the story had taken a new turn. The Baagandji people who were native to the area also took up the word 'kangaroo' but they used it to speak of horses, which, of course, they had never seen before some came prancing off the ships from England. We make a lot of the first encounter between Europeans and the strange animals of their distant imperial possessions but perhaps we don't spend enough time considering the oddities that sheep, cows and horses must have been to the local people.

But the most amazing fact of all is yet to come: no linguist was able to record the word 'kangaroo' again until 1972. So the word remained concealed for some two hundred years after the first English visitors noted it down.

But if the enormous deserts of Australia could absorb the great gold reef or a rare species of ant and they could certainly absorb a word and keep it hidden for over two centuries, the somewhat more manicured pastures of English literature could not resist displaying this new discovery. The kangaroo first appears in English literature as early as 1794 in Robert Southey's poem 'Elinor'. This was one of his collection of 'Botany Bay Eclogues', the first serious English poems to make any effort to summon up or describe the Australian experience. In this poem the exiled convict imagines the English landscape, well cultivated, inhabited by 'fearless redbreasts' and the English soundscape animated by the 'hollow tone' of the rook. In

Australia however things are different. The landscape is 'pathless', unbroken by plough, 'undelved by hand / Of patient rustic.' The soundscape has no 'lowing herds':

> And for the music of the bleating flocks,
> Alone is heard the kangaroo's sad note
> Deepening in the distance.

Southey was far more celebrated in his own day than he is now and it is said that he once went to dinner with a provincial family who were thrilled to make the acquaintance of an eminent literary man. They were eager to impress him and so ordered in the most expensive, luxurious and fashionable commodity they could think of and this happened to be tea. Unfortunately they had no idea what to do with it and served it boiled as a vegetable. Whether Southey, presented with such an unpalatable meal – much as the nabobs of the East India Company were sometimes presented with sardines and tinned peaches bought from the Europe shop and served in chamber pots by anxious-to-please native princes – was able to eat it I don't know. One other thing about Southey is that he was a great cat fancier and was pretty flamboyant in naming them. His tabby was His Serene Highness, the Archduke Rumpelstiltzchen, Marquis MacBum, Earl Tomlemange, Baron Raticide, Waouhler and Skaratsch. Calling him in for the night must have been quite a feat of memory although he probably didn't go out much as in Southey's garden lurked the fearsome (although more plebeianly named) Hurlyburlybuss.

What I do know, however, is that Southey's idea of a kangaroo was as vague as his probably mythical hosts' idea of a cup of tea. Given the period we are speaking of it is highly unlikely that even the most remote household would not have known how to make a cup of tea – after all by 1821 William Cobbett was railing that excessive tea drinking was proving the ruin of the English working class, which is an interesting and typically contrary spin on what was to become a common Victorian theme, although later moralists seemed to think that beer was slightly more of a problem. In 'Elinor' a patterning which contrasts aspects of England (the remembered home) with aspects of Australia (the experienced place of exile) demands that features found in one are balanced against features found in another. At one level it probably didn't matter to Southey what a kangaroo was or what it sounded like. It probably didn't matter if it didn't make any sound at all: his readers (unless they had been out with Cook) wouldn't know any different. No, what was wanted was an exotic animal and, as early as 1794, when an English writer wanted to sum up the Australian scene in one word it looks as if 'kangaroo' would fit the bill. But I am truly nostalgic for a world in which kangaroos call plaintively to each other across the red centre.

By 1804 things had not improved and the even more obscure poet Charles Dibdin ventured a kangaroo in his bizarre work 'The Harmonic Preceptor; a Didactic Poem in Three Parts'. This engagingly cranky poem is an attempt to teach the principles of musical composition in verse. The piece is, not surprisingly, virtually unreadable but, towards the end, a kangaroo hops in and is used as the image of an oddity:

> Modern singing, were't not to true taste so injurious,
> Might be really encouraged like any thing curious,
> An invisible girl, or a young kangaroo,
> Or pigs without heads, or a calf that has two,
> A hare beating a drum, or a crocodile stuffed,
> Or any thing else the news-papers have puffed,
> Which obtains on the public by sly advertising,
> And are really wonderful thought, and surprising.

If for Southey the kangaroo is a kind of marsupial ball and chain on the convict's dream world, for Dibdin it is straightforwardly a wonder and, most likely, not even a real animal. Note how he matches it with freak show exhibits. The kind of thing that he had in mind was, no doubt, this advertisement from *The Times* of 16th November 1791:

> The Wonderful Kangaroo from Botany Bay. A most beautiful and healthy animal in a state of perfect tameness, and entirely free from any blemish, is now exhibiting at No. 31, the Top of the Hay Market. Admittance One Shilling each. It is not easy to describe that peculiarity of attitudes and uncommon

proportion of parts which so strikingly distinguishes the Kangaroo from all other Creatures; and it may be presumed, that few who possess a taste for science, or a laudable curiousity of inspecting Wonders of Nature, will resist embracing the only opportunity hitherto afforded in Europe of viewing this singular Native of the Southern Hemisphere, in its natural state of vigour and activity.

When you think that a farm worker earned about seven shillings and six pence (37.5p) per week in the 1790s a shilling (5p) to see a *kangaroo* looks a fairly steep price. Obviously it was too steep for Southey who might have done a better job of describing kangaroos in 'Elinor' if he had got himself down to the Haymarket. In the year before this exhibition (1790) Alexander Weir was advertising the 'extraordinary Quadruped called THE CUNQUROO ... being the first that was ever brought to Britain' at his natural history museum in Edinburgh. By 1796 the Royal Navy had named one of its sloops *Kangaroo* and this ship did good service throughout the Napoleonic wars, being finally sold off in 1818. Fittingly, it enjoyed at least one cruise into southern waters as it was the ship that lugged away the debris from the abandoned settlement on Norfolk Island in 1814. I wonder what the figurehead looked like. The Royal Navy doesn't, alas, have a record of it.

Things were looking up by 1810 with the publication of Sir Walter Scott's posthumous collection of Anna Seward's *Poetical Works*. In her 'Elegy on Captain Cook' Seward chose to imagine a somewhat more positive version of Australia and, in particular, was moved to situate the new continent within a peculiarly European mythology:

> Next Fauna treads, in youthful beauty's pride
> A playful Kangroo bounding by her side
> Around the Nymph her beauteous Pois display
> Their varied plumes, and trill the dulcet lay;
> A Giant-bat, with leathern wings outspread,
> Umbrella light, hangs quiv'ring o'er her head.

The Pois and Giant-bat make interesting companions. If by giant-bat Seward means the creatures which stream from

Sydney's Botanical Gardens every evening and circle like a pack of autogyro-riding Alsatian dogs while you are trying to enjoy your gourmet pizza on Circular Quay I wouldn't call it 'umbrella light'. She also obviously thinks that Pois are some kind of bird – in fact they are feathery balls which are twirled during Maori dances. But, in spite of these errors Anna Seward plainly knew what a 'Kangroo' was. If Seward's poem had appeared during her lifetime she would have pipped Southey for the honour of being the first English poet to write about kangaroos. Scott however prudently added an editorial note:

> The Kangroo is an animal peculiar to those climates. It is perpetually jumping along on its hind legs, its fore legs being too short to be used in the manner of other quadrupeds.

Scott's caution may have been unnecessary. In fact, by adding this note he may well be showing that he had misunderstood what Seward was trying to do. We see in her poem not a wanton casting around for the exotic and the marvellous for its own sake but a genuine attempt to bring the strange wonders of Australian nature into a literary setting which would have been deeply familiar to her readers. The neo-classical picture she paints is not designed to display the odd but rather to offer the reader a very easily accommodated and comforting scene. The mythological image offers the reader the opportunity to understand this new world in the terms of the old and thus the 'Kangroo' is, to an extent, tamed.

It is instructive to contrast these various false starts with the treatment of kangaroos in a somewhat later poem, John Abraham Heraud's *The Judgement of the Flood*. This was published in 1857 by which time the public was much more familiar with the creature. An infallible sign of that familiarity is the fact that Charles Dickens reports Mrs Micawber as speaking of 'the habits of the kangaroo' in *David Copperfield* (1850) and Dickens's grasp of his readers' taste and understanding was so sure that he would not have done that if he thought that he would only succeed in puzzling them. Heraud accounts for the kangaroo thus:

> The Kangaroo, on its hind legs sustained,
> And moving fast, high-bounding and afar,
> Its fore too brief, and but as hands employed,
> To dig with, or to feed.

This, as you can see, is pretty accurate and if we can set aside the interesting theology that has kangaroos hopping up the gangplank into Noah's Ark – although in 1933 the Australian national poet A. B. 'Banjo' Paterson wrote a splendid book of children's verse, *The Animals Noah Forgot*, suggesting that he knew better and including an account of digging contest in which the wonderful Weary Willie the wombat king beats Bristling Billy the porcupine (Billy hits an ants' nest and stops for lunch) – this poem does demonstrate a new confidence in dealing with this particular animal for a predominantly British readership.

Perhaps predictably, the earliest Australian poems to mention kangaroos do a better job of actually imaging the creatures but they post-date the English examples cited so far (except for Heraud) and, very largely, situate the Australian experience within well-worn European forms. John Dunmore Lang's 'Australian Hymn' (written 'For the Native Youth of the Colony') imagines the empty continent finally populated by:

> The rudest mortal under Heaven,
> Stern nature's long-forgotten child!
> Compatriot of the tall Emu,
> The Wombat and the Kangaroo!

Here the aboriginal human takes his place along side the exotic fauna and stumbles along with them until the civilising influences of Britain make themselves felt. This brings in a theme which is apparent in much colonial discourse but which is not always as readily acknowledged as it might be and that is that the animals of a colonised country or continent become just as much the subjects of the colonising power as the human inhabitants.

In 'The Kangaroo', written no later than 1823 by the superbly named Barron Field, a valiant attempt is made to see the kangaroo in its own right and to recognise it explicitly as 'Thou Spirit of Australia.' However, Field also has his eye, probably not unwisely from a commercial point of view, on an English reader who will have no idea, or very little idea, of what he is trying to describe and his hymn of praise to kangaroos attempts to disentangle the curious realities of the animal's physiology from the 'Sphynx', the 'Minotaure', 'Pegasus' or the 'hippogriff'. Field bravely tries to establish an aesthetic for the kangaroo that makes it, in itself, a justification for Australia:

> Better-proportion'd animal,
> More graceful or ethereal,
> Was never follow'd by the hound,
> With fifty steps to one bound.
> Thou can'st not be amended: no;
> Be as thou art; thou best art so,
> When sooty swans are once more rare,
> And duck-moles the Museum's care,
> Be still the glory of this land,
> Happiest Work of finest Hand!

Field (who was a judge) was far from happy with his posting to Sydney, and the kangaroo (and it appears the thought of setting his hounds after it) provided a bright spot in an existence where there was precious little to please him. His final verdict on Australia 'where's no past tense the ignorant present's all' sums up the problem of the European in a continent that appeared to be, in European terms at least, empty.

Of course, Field's caution in ensuring that his English readers understand that the curious proportions of the kangaroo are as God made them and not the work of mythologist or taxidermist can be seen as justified when we consider the reaction to the first duck-billed platypus (duck-mole as Field calls it) that appeared, stuffed, in Britain round about 1798. It was highly controversial and widely considered to be a fake although by 16th April 1846 *The Times* carried a notice offering a stuffed example for sale and, in 1851, a stuffed platypus featured in the Great Exhibition which, as *The Times* pointed out, showed that it must be real:

THE ORNITHORHYNCHUS. The attention of naturalists has been recently much arrested by two specimens of that extraordinary animal the Ornithorhyncus or duck-billed platypus, exhibited in the west nave (sec. 16) of the Exhibition. It is a native of Australia and bears some resemblance to the beaver and the otter, with a fur similar to those creatures. The head is rather flat, and the mouth furnished with a bill like that of a duck; it is notwithstanding this marvellous incongruity a very pretty looking animal. When first sent to this country it was received by zoologists with caution amounting to suspicion; nor was it till one or two more specimens arrived from Governor Hunter (we believe, and addressed to Sir Joseph Banks) that naturalists were ready to allow that the beak was naturally attached to the body. Sir Henry Halford also devoted much time to the investigation of this subject, and succeeded in establishing the fact of its reality – a satisfactory instance of the progress and accuracy of scientific application. The Great Exhibition has been the means of placing this great wonder before the public. It is exhibited by Mr. G. Ellis of Fore-street.

However, as late as 1884, when the mystery was finally cleared up, it was still considered 'a fable' that the platypus laid eggs. The answer was eventually provided by the scientist William Caldwell whose expedition (with a team of aboriginal hunters) to solve the problem resulted in the deaths of some 1,300 echidnas and a similar number of platypuses. It is probable that the populations of both animals have never fully recovered from this massacre.

So although the kangaroo was better known than other Australian mammals we should not be surprised by Field's anxiousness and the lines of thought he naturally turned to when trying to describe it. What is also interesting is the relative archaism of Field's style and form. Again, it feels as if the intention is to familiarise the reader with the unfamiliarity of Australian animals through the use of a very familiar style of poetic diction.

Also worth catching is that elegiac note and the fear that something might happen to jeopardise the long-term future of

Illustration 9
Nature conservation in colonial Australia: a platypus hunt

Australian species. You hear it later in the century in George Williams's 'A Plea of Despair' written, as the epigraph notes, 'before reservations were made for native game':

> Search where in thundering squadrons the bison was found,
> Never again on the prairie his hoof shall resound;
> Helpless marsupial soon shall sink into the ground.
>
> Thus shall the opossum and wombat and wallaby fade;
> Nature shall sink into silence and gloomiest shade;
> Rustle of gorgeous plume shall not brighten the glade.

This rather moving poem – although as with all of this kind of work the animal names still hit with a jolt – shows one of the problems that the British had in coming to terms with Australia and its creatures. This was a country that, in their minds at least, had been settled not conquered. There was, therefore, not quite the same attitude to the local animals that there had been in

India and Africa. Here a tradition of big game hunting had grown up alongside the development of an imperial ruling class. It is not hard to understand why this should be: in killing lions and tigers the colonists were representing both to themselves and to their native subjects the very processes of colonisation. You master the people and then you master the animals. But in Australia the situation seems somewhat different and there does not seem to have been any particular tradition of hunting in the Indo–African sense.

This may have been because Australian animals are not particularly dangerous. At least not the big mammals: the crocodiles are nasty and so are the spiders and snakes. So in stalking the mammals you don't get the largely imaginary *frisson* that one might eat you. It may also have been that the early ruling class in Australia simply didn't (because of its remoteness) develop the critical mass that is probably needed for a good hunting culture to develop. But I think it is because of the nature of the settlement: there was no need to tame the Australian animals because there had not really been any need to tame the people. But this is not to say that both people and animals were not slaughtered in appalling numbers. They were: the officers of the penal colony on Sarah Island amused themselves by blasting away at kangaroos and catching wombats and echidnas to eat (the wombats they spit roasted like suckling pigs, the echidnas they stuffed with sage and onion). The symbolic function of the slaughter was different though and neither am I aware that the plight of Indian, American and African animals in the face of breech-loading firearms was picked up by anyone before George Williams.

Kangaroos had arrived in England, dead, with Captain Cook's ships and alive not much after as specimens obtained for George III's private zoo, and these did extremely well. Stubbs, working, it appears, from an inflated hide, painted the first English one in 1772 or 1773 to the commission of Joseph Banks. An earlier image and the first in Europe of a kangaroo-like animal, the New Guinean Brown Pademelon, had appeared in the Amsterdam edition of Cornelis de Bruin's *Reizen over*

Moskovie door Persie en India (1714), the author having seen the creature in Java. The hide Stubbs worked from probably belonged to the very same kangaroo whose skull was being analysed by the pioneering surgeon John Hunter at much the same time. Interestingly enough Stubbs placed his kangaroo not in Windsor Great Park where kangaroos were actually to live but in what appears to be a pretty good approximation of an Australian landscape. I'd like to know where he got the model for that – presumably from Banks himself or maybe from the sketches of kangaroos produced by Sydney Parkinson, the illustrator who accompanied Banks on Cook's voyage. By 1804, the royal kangaroos had bred for ten years and had made themselves pretty comfortable in the English landscape and climate. In that year William Bingley noted that the Windsor Great Park kangaroos were 'in a great degree naturalised to England'. Sir Joseph Banks himself farmed kangaroos on his estate at Revesby in Lincolnshire – thus setting a fashion for kangaroo keeping in that wonderful county which persisted into the 1960s. As late as 1829 there was still a kangaroo in the Tower Menagerie and an advertisement of much the same time for that attraction refers to 'a pair of kangaroos (male and female)' adding intriguingly that they were 'bred in Windsor Great Park'. So although Australian animals posed real difficulties to the categories of European zoology (much as Native American languages were to challenge traditional models of grammar and philology in the early years of the last century) they were soon appropriated as specimens, as tourist attractions, as metaphors, and as pets. By the end of the century kangaroos were seen as such a distinctively British thing that the Florentine government sent a mission to England to try to purchase one for the Grand Duke.

The kangaroos in Windsor Great Park had some interesting neighbours. George III continued the royal tradition of keeping a menagerie that had started in 1235 when the Holy Roman Emperor Frederick II gave Henry II of England three 'leopards' (which were probably lions) and these were then housed in the Tower of London. In fact, George and his family had several menageries and royal beasts were not only to be found in

Windsor Great Park – which collection had actually been started by the Duke of Cumberland. There was the Royal Menagerie at the Tower, a collection at Kew kept near the building now known as Queen Charlotte's Cottage and Princess Fredrica, wife to Frederick Augustus (the original 'Grand Old Duke of York') kept a fine collection at her palace in Oatlands Park. Her zoo largely consisted of parrots, never-ridden horses and a pack of dogs. She spent her time with these animals when the Duke was 'away at the wars' and when Oatlands House caught fire in 1794 she kept a cool head and personally supervised the evacuation of her pets.

But the real star of George's collection at Windsor, which included a lion, a tiger and a zebra, was the cheetah presented to the King by George Pigot, Governor of Madras, complete with two Indian handlers. Pigot commissioned Stubbs to paint this animal too but the actual painting shows a less than happy incident. In order to put the creature through its paces a palisade was erected and a stag placed inside the enclosure thus formed. The cheetah, still complete with two Indian handlers, was then sent into the circle to hunt the stag. This it determinedly set its face against and, in the picture, the Indian handlers are rather desperately pointing it at its intended prey. Anyone who has ever tried to get a cat to do anything will immediately understand their problem. Meanwhile the stag looks all feisty and monarch of the glenny in the background. It appears that the Indian handlers did finally get the cheetah going but the stag simply took it on its antlers and tossed it over the palisade fence. At which point the experiment was, not unwisely, abandoned. One last thing: if Windsor Great Park was partly populated by kangaroos it did its bit to populate Australia. The herd of red deer that was released in the Brisbane Valley in 1873 came from Windsor Great Park. The deer are still in Queensland but although the kangaroos have long gone from Windsor we can console ourselves that the Derbyshire wallabies, in spite of occasional rumours to the contrary, are still going strong and, I am told, becoming increasingly urbanised.

And this is where we return to wombats, for where kangaroos

bound wombats will surely snuffle along behind, their pouches facing backward to prevent them from becoming filled with the loose soil of the outback. Or, indeed, with the heavy London clay of Cheyne Walk. It is now time to meet Top and, along with Top, a host of other captive animals some exotic and some not and a collection of human beings who are more exotic than most.

THE DUKE OF EDINBURGH'S WOMBAT

HIS ROYAL HIGHNESS THE PRINCE ALFRED ERNEST ALBERT, KG, KT, KP, CGMG, GCIE, GCVO, RVO, PC, Duke of Saxe-Coburg and Gotha, Duke of Edinburgh, Earl of Kent, Earl of Ulster was born in 1844, the fourth child of Queen Victoria and Prince Albert. He was also their second son, which meant that although they had managed to create the 'heir and spare' something had to be done with and by the spare while his older brother the future King Edward VII was groomed, not altogether successfully, for the throne. And what better for a growing boy than to carry on the developing tradition of a connection between the Royal Family and the Royal Navy? To this end he joined up in 1856 and four years later was posted to *HMS Euryalus* as a midshipman.

But Prince Alfred was a notably cheerful and vigorous young man and was extremely serious about his nautical career. He clearly saw it as far more than simply a pastime designed to keep him out of mischief. In 1862 diplomatic protocols meant that he narrowly avoided the thankless task of becoming King of Greece and, instead, he stayed on in the navy diligently doing (as England expected) his duties and attracting more honours: the Order of the Black Eagle (Prussia), the Order of the Golden Fleece (Spain), the Annunziata (Italy), the Legion of Honour (France), the Order of St Stephen (Austria), the Order of St Andrew (Russia) and the Ostamnieh (the Ottoman Empire). He must have been quite a sight when the sun was low in the sky and he had all his stars on. In 1866 he was promoted to Captain and given command of the frigate *HMS Galatea*.

In January 1867 *Galatea* set off for a voyage around the world carrying Prince Alfred on what was the first major overseas royal visit. He was the first member of the Royal family to visit the colonies and, I believe, the first member of the Royal family to cross the Equator. The trip was watched with great fascination and pleasure in Britain and *The Times* reported regularly on the *Galatea*'s progress and on any interesting doings of the Prince and his crew along the way.

Illustration 10
Prince Alfred about to embark on a kangaroo hunt

The Duke's voyage finally took him to Australia where he stayed for five months with much acclaim – there was even a dance craze for the Prince Alfred waltz. Starting in Adelaide, he visited Melbourne, Sydney, Brisbane, and Hobart before returning to Sydney. But here disaster struck. While attending a charity picnic at Clontarf in aid of a sailor's charity the Prince was shot in the back – as he was making his donation it appears or maybe as he was about to go to look at a display of aboriginal dancing, accounts vary – by Henry James O'Farrell, a self-declared Fenian. There is some doubt about whether he was actually part of any organisation as he was probably a fantasist and the internal politics of that part of Australia were, at that time, strongly marked by generalised sectarian tension and violence between the Protestant and Catholic communities. O'Farrell claimed to be seeking to avenge the hanging of three members of the Fenian Brotherhood for the murder of a Manchester policeman. The would-be assassin narrowly escaped lynching on the spot – 'Cut him to pieces with scissors' screeched the women – but was subsequently executed, although the Prince made earnest and sincere pleas for clemency.

If at around this time intrepid Victorian ladies were learning the value of a good thick skirt as they plunged through the thorns of the veldt or the clinging rain forests of West Africa, the Duke now learned the value of a good thick pair of trousers – or rather braces. O'Farrell's dastardly bullet struck the Duke in the back but the solidity of his leather braces – some accounts say their gutta percha and brass buckles (which, I have to say, I much prefer as a picture) – saved him from serious injury and, although the bullet lodged between his ribs, the wound was not mortal and he was soon nursed back to health. However, in spite of the excellent care he received, at the hands of two nurses who had been trained by Florence Nightingale herself as it happens, it was deemed expedient that he return to England for further medical attention and this he did, in full command of *Galatea*, leaving Sydney on 4th April 1868 and arriving in Portsmouth on 26th June of the same year.

Now, why is all this of any interest? The reason is that Prince Alfred was, like many of his Royal ancestors, quite an animal fancier and collected, according to *The Times*, a 'large and varied collection of colonial birds and animals' while he was in Australia where he also did a fair bit of possum shooting.

His most famous pet was an elephant which he acquired while visiting India on the resumption of the *Galatea*'s cruise when it was deemed that he was fit enough to complete the ambitious itinerary. The elephant was quite a favourite and was present when the Duke finally laid down command of *HMS Galatea*. In fact, it was guest of honour when the Duke left his old ship for the last time. *The Times* described the event:

Illustration 11
*Prince Alfred's Australian
menagerie. Note: there is no wombat*

...the crew, hauled by the elephant and preceded by the band of the Royal Marines, marched in procession to the Mechanics' Institute where a dinner had been provided for the men.

But this triumphant homecoming had a tragic end. James Paton was one of *Galatea*'s Marines and when the Duke left the *Galatea* he travelled on with him – as his elephant keeper to be precise. But poor Paton was killed by the elephant at Newton Abbot in June 1871 as *The Times* recorded:

The Duke of Edinburgh's Elephant – The inquest on the unfortunate James Paton who was killed while travelling with the Duke of Edinburgh from Plymouth to London, by train, was held at the Queen's Hotel near the Newton station, on Saturday evening before Mr. M. Michelmore and a respectable jury. The deceased was a native of Glasgow, and had been on board the *Galatea* with the elephant 17 months, the animal on no occasion showing any ferocity. Mr. L. Bartlett, from the Zoological Gardens, and an assistant keeper travelled in the horse box with the animal and keeper. The elephant became very restive on leaving Plymouth station, and broke down the partition separating them from the animal. The deceased Paton endeavoured, with the others, to pacify it, and it is supposed the elephant pressed him against the side of the carriage with his tusk. Bartlett and his assistant heard him cry out, but could not get to him as he was on the other side of the box, and the elephant was very restive. He must have died almost immediately. There were no bones broken, but there was a mark of a bruise on his chest. Lieutenant Adolphus St. George from the *Galatea*, attended with others to give evidence. The jury returned a verdict of "Accidental Death." The Duke of Edinburgh saw the body on Saturday.

What a nightmare. Imagine being stuck in a railway carriage between Plymouth and Newton Abbot at any time and then add the job of pacifying an angry elephant. And this was only a day after the triumphant procession.

Two significant things emerge from this report. The first is that the elephant had been on the *Galatea* for seventeen months. That would mean the Duke had acquired it in late 1869 or early 1870. At that time he was in India, which is a good place for acquiring elephants. Indeed, the reports of the Duke's activities there make much mention of his interest in elephants (as was also the case when he visited South Africa where a pass is still named after him) and his participation, with elephants, in tiger hunts. But what on earth do you do with an elephant on a smallish warship? And for seventeen months too. It is not difficult to believe that the crew's cheers when the elephant left were as much relief to see the broad grey back of him as anything else. And not least, because of what can be guessed from a painting of the Galatea on its cruise. This was done by Oswald Brierly whom the Duke took with him as the Galatea's artist – Prince Alfred didn't believe in doing things by halves. This shows the ship in a pretty rough sea and at an angle which would have had the cups off the table if nothing else.

Trying to look after an elephant (especially one that was upset by the much less alarming jolts of a train journey) in that cannot have been a laughing matter. The second is the presence

Illustration 12
The Galatea *at sea (with an elephant on board)*

of Mr Bartlett and his assistant. I take this to mean that the Duke intended to donate the elephant to the zoo and I assume that in spite of its unfortunate attack on Paton (which may well have been an accident) that is where it ended its days.

If the Duke's elephant did go to the zoo it would probably have joined Queen Victoria's elephant 'Prince Albert' who had arrived out of the blue one day in 1840, having been sent as a gift by an anonymous donor in Calcutta (where there is still an elephant statue dedicated to the Prince Consort), and was sent straight to the zoo. This shows how the times had changed: a real Hanoverian would have let him rumble happily around Windsor Great Park. Unfortunately we don't know the name of the Prince's elephant but I doubt if it was as magnificent as that borne by the last Royal elephant to be kept in the Royal elephant house in Bangkok: Prasawat Adundtet Paho Puni Pom Nam Nata Balami Tudiya Sawekali Khamotpan Nophat Belom Khamala Satnat Wisutamon Sapatbonkon Laksinat Khatchien

Katradtad Soyamrasdaon Suwadipratsit Pratanagundshon Nitnitbunyatikan Patratmintatrat Bhapitratsan Sakhundpha. 'Prince Albert' is nowhere before that and even Southey's cat seems a positive commoner.

One other Royal animal that intrudes here and is too good to be forgotten is Obaysch the hippopotamus who was given to the zoo in 1850 after an eventful journey from the White Nile. Obaysch became the focus of a cult. The Queen visited him regularly, you could buy silver hippopotami as souvenirs and the *Hippopotamus Polka*, with sheet music showing a rather demure young lady being squired round the floor by a hippo in white tie, gave rise to a dance craze. *Punch* wrote about him regularly, Dickens complained that he (Obaysch) was monopolising the attention of visitors to the zoo – they came by the thousand to see him and an engraving of Obaysch c.1852 does indeed show a pretty large crowd pressed to the bars of his enclosure.

Illustration 13
Obaysch taking a bath

When he died in 1878 *Punch* published a memorial verse. Obaysch was perhaps the first of a number of zoo-based cults and wombats would shortly follow.

But, to get back to the Duke's elephant: if my assumption about the zoo is right then that could be a most interesting snippet of information – interesting because the Duke also had a wombat. This was presented to him when the *Galatea* visited Hobart, as reported in *The Times* on his return in June 1868:

> In Tasmania he procured a very fine wombat which was presented to him by Lady Dry wife of the Chief Secretary of that colony; this wombat was so tame and docile that it soon became a general favourite with all on board the *Galatea*.

There is actually a photograph of the Duke arriving at Government House in Hobart and I would love to think that inside the rather impressive building was a little wombat waiting to meet its new owner.

Illustration 14
Prince Alfred arriving at Government House on the day he was presented with his wombat.

There is also a stereoscopic photograph of the *Galatea* at anchor in Hobart harbour but, unfortunately, there is no way of knowing whether this was before or after the wombat came into the Duke's hands.

Illustration 15
HMS Galatea *in Hobart harbour*

But while I am in fanciful mood I would like to think that if we could pierce the sides of the vessel we would see a wombat sitting on a sailor's knee.

Now, the Duke got the wombat shortly before his fateful visit to Sydney and his enforced return to England in June 1868. What happened to the wombat? It may well have gone to the zoo as probably did the elephant. But did it? When the Duke returned in 1871 he was leaving the *Galatea* which was to be paid off and dismantled. He therefore had plenty of time to order his affairs and these affairs included the problem of what to do with an elephant. When he returned in 1868 things were different. He had been the victim of a vicious attack and suffered a nasty injury. Politicians and courtiers would have been clucking all round him. He was also a man with a keen sense of duty and would, no doubt, have been far from pleased that his tour had been seriously disrupted even though he was not in mortal danger from the gunshot wound. It just might be that the disposal of a wombat would not have been a top priority. It may also have been that one of the *Galatea*'s crew had taken the wombat on and now had to do something with it. I am sure the wombat did arrive here. A man who could keep an elephant on a ship for seventeen months could certainly have kept a wombat – and other birds and animals from that extensive collection – for just two. Could it be that it was disposed of through the London trade in exotic animals? If so, who next bought it?

This is all speculation of course but there were not many wombats about in England in the late 1860s and it's interesting that one turned up for sale shortly after we can safely assume that one had arrived on a Royal Navy vessel.

PRE-RAPHAELITES AND WOMBATS

The facts are quite simple.

In September 1869 the Pre-Raphaelite painter Dante Gabriel Rossetti bought himself a wombat and called him Top. In November 1869 the wombat died.

What is there to say about such a little life? We don't know how old Top was when he arrived in the Rossetti household. We don't really know if he had voyaged from Australia or was born in the teeming confines of Jamrach's exotic animal shop on the Ratcliff Highway in the East End of London although this latter possibility is very unlikely given the conditions wombats require for breeding. All we know is that for three months an exotic marsupial lived in Chelsea and captured the imaginations˙not only of Rossetti but also of the literary and artistic world that circled around and sometimes visited his darkened Cheyne Walk villa.

We can start to think about what to say in three different ways. We can see how Top fitted into the private zoo that Rossetti maintained in his spacious garden beside the Thames. We can fill in the details of Top's life as we have it from the letters and sketches of Rossetti and his friends. We can consider what Top meant to Rossetti and how a tiny Australian became part of a very English *ménage a trois* between Rossetti, William Morris and his wife Jane.

The year 1857 marks one possible beginning of the story. In this year Rossetti gathered his forces, including Edward Burne-Jones, Arthur Hughes, William Morris, Hungerford Pollen, Val Prinsep and Spencer Stanhope, and set out for Oxford where he had been commissioned (on a no-fee basis) to provide murals for the new Oxford Union debating hall (now the Union library). At this point Morris had just shifted over from possible patron to disciple and this shift in relationship, I believe, was partly at the root of the subsequent trials of his relationship with Rossetti. Morris was a rich young man with an income from investments but he had a strong artistic bent that he first expressed as a collector. In 1856 he had bought Arthur Hughes's painting *April Love* (which he always referred to as his favourite Pre-Raphaelite work) for thirty pounds. When Burne-Jones (then plain Ned Jones) took Morris's cheque round to Hughes's studio the painter recalled that his 'chief feeling was then surprise at an Oxford student buying pictures'. At the time Rossetti wrote to William Allingham informing him that 'Morris is a millionaire and buys pictures. He bought Hughes's *April Love*.' I can't help catching a note of indecently eager anticipation here especially as Morris also purchased five of Rossetti's watercolours depicting medieval themes. Later that year Ford Madox Brown recorded that 'Rossetti brought his ardent admirer Morris of Oxford, who bought my little hay field for forty guineas'. (Morris later gave the painting back to Brown as payment for some work at Kelmscott – this is the painting called *The Hayfield* now in the Tate.)

When he saw *April Love* Morris wrote to Burne-Jones asking him to 'go and nobble that picture called *April Love* as soon as possible lest anybody else should buy it.' I find the picture of the young Morris with a pocket full of cash and a heart full of hope trying to break into the world of the artists he so admires wonderfully touching. It is so profoundly human that it catches in the throat. Especially when, with hindsight, we know what private pain was in store for him and how he bore it with such decency, magnanimity and integrity.

Given the fact that an artist as inexperienced as Morris (although a critic as eminent as Coventry Patmore perceptively remarked on his 'real feeling for peculiarly architectural painting') was working on the Union paintings, it is not surprising that they lasted less than twelve months as the walls had not been properly prepared for fresco. Rather surprisingly perhaps, Morris, Rossetti and Ford Madox Brown were commissioned five years later to decorate the Old Hall at Queen's College Cambridge and did a much better job. The chaotic period that ensued during the young painters' residence resulted in two things which were to have a crucial bearing on the lives of all the humans and non-humans on whom this narrative touches: Rossetti and his young friends drew wombats and Morris met Jane Burden.

★★★

A wombat had been born in the Zoological Society's Gardens in Regent's Park in 1856 and wombats had lived there for what could be described in John Gould's *The Mammals of Australia* (1855) as 'a long time'. In fact, the first wombat had arrived there on 26th October 1830. Rossetti loved the zoo and had been a frequent visitor since his childhood when he would go there with his family. On one such occasion his sister Christina was badly bitten by a peccary. In adult life he would take his friends for walks there often meeting at what he called 'the Wombat's Lair'. This was easy to find being in the north-east corner of the park in the angle formed by the Outer Walk and the Broad Walk which run round the zoo's perimeter and between the Monkey House and the Falcon Aviary.

But in fact, it was Dante Gabriel's brother and sister William and Christina who first discovered the joys of wombats and, as William told Christina's biographer, Mackenzie Bell 'from us (especially myself) Gabriel, Burne-Jones, and other wombat enthusiasts ensued'. On 18th August 1858 Christina wrote to William describing a trip to the zoo when 'the blind wombat and the neighbouring porcupine broke forth into short-lived hostilities, but apparently without permanent results'. William later misremembered his dates and thought that it was as late as 1858 that he and Christina first saw the wombat:

> ...our steps led us toward a certain enclosure hitherto unknown to us, and little scrutinised by most visitors. Christina, who had as good an eye for 'a beast' as Dante Gabriel, caught sight of '*phascolomys ursinus*' a second before

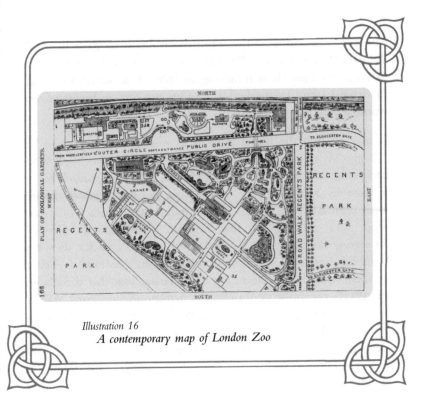

Illustration 16
A contemporary map of London Zoo

myself, and exclaimed, 'Oh look at that delightful object!' I soon instructed my brother what part of the Zoological Gardens he should go to in order to contemplate the form and proportions of the wombat; he, I surmise, afterwards put up Burne-Jones to the same quest.

Actually, this must have been in 1857 at the latest but the point is that the first entry of wombats into the Rossetti household preceded the advent of Top. In 1859 G. P. Boyce noted that:

> Rossetti came and we went to Tennyson Street and picked up Fanny, and thence to Zoological Gardens, where he wanted to draw a fawn for his Magdalen drawing [this, I assume, is the work entitled *Mary Magdalene at the door of Simon the Pharisee*]. We stayed there 3 or 4 hours, most amused by the brown bear, wombat and some owls.

On 24th July 1862 a hairy-nosed wombat was added to the zoo's collection and in 1863 this was joined by two common wombats who came all the way from Melbourne Zoo. In 1867 William Rossetti noted 'The black wombat very fat' after a visit to Regent's Park. It is tempting to think that when, in 1872, Blanchard Jerrold remarked 'I have known human lovers of the wombat', he had the Rossettis and their friends in mind.

It may be that the initial interest in wombats was sparked by Thomas Woolner, one of the Pre-Raphaelite Brotherhood who had emigrated to Australia in 1852 on a fruitless search for a fortune as a gold digger and whose communications home were regularly read aloud at PRB gatherings. James Collinson, who was another of the original Brotherhood, painted *Answering the Emigrant's Letter* (1850) which actually shows a humblish interior in which a letter from Australia is being considered and it is interesting to speculate that this stimulated the PRB's reception of Woolner's correspondence. Ford Madox Brown's painting *The Last of England* was an ironic image of himself and his wife Emma but it was inspired by Woolner's departure when William and Dante Gabriel Rossetti and Holman Hunt as well as the Browns accompanied Woolner on the first stage of the long journey south. Woolner found neither gold nor fame and came back to England in 1854 where his career suddenly took off after all. Later on, the original PRB had a more successful Australian foray when, in 1905–07, Holman Hunt's painting *The Light of the World* was taken on a tour of the dominions including South Africa, Canada, New Zealand and Australia. In Western Australia alone 104,000 people went to see it in eight days. This is an astonishing figure given that the population of Australia was, at that time, about 3.8 million. Did the best part of three per cent of the total really file past Hunt's image in those few days? A contemporary photograph of the crowds in front of the picture when it was shown at Melbourne suggests they may well have done.

In fact, it was well before Top had become a kind of heraldic beast for Rossetti's Cheyne Walk court that Christina had twice invoked the Regent's Park wombat in her masterpiece, *Goblin Market*. This was first published in 1859. The goblins appear in various guises:

"Buy from us with a golden curl"

Illustration 17
Rossetti's frontispiece to Goblin Market:
spot the wombat

One had a cat's face,
One whisked a tail,
One tramped at a rat's pace,
One crawled like a snail,
One like a wombat prowled obtuse and furry,
One like a ratel tumbled hurry skurry.

They are:

> Cat-like and rat-like,
> Ratel- and Wombat-like

Rossetti illustrated this passage as a frontispiece to Christina's *Goblin Market and Other Poems* which came out in 1862. The wombat is clearly visible in this and the others of Rossetti's images for this publication although, zoologically speaking, it is rather generic.

In fact, none of the early attempts to illustrate Goblin Market get the wombat right: Laurence Houseman's 1893 version has the goblins so swathed in hats and cloaks that it is difficult to tell one from the other, the late Pre-Raphaelite follower Agnes Rope's 1905 effort has a curious creature which, by a process of elimination, must be the wombat, Margaret Tarrant's illustrated edition of 1912 has a clearly recognisable owl but nothing like a wombat. By 1933 Arthur Rackham was drawing something like a rat. Christina's own pencil sketch of the Regent's Park wombat has survived as has a sketch by William Rossetti but, unfortunately, it is unclear whether this is an image of a zoo-based wombat or of Top.

So when Dante Gabriel led his troops to Oxford they were enthused not only with the romance of life as painters and medievalists engaged upon the most important work of restoring the beauty of the Middle Ages to the city of lost causes but also with the romance of wombats. When the windows of the Union were whitewashed to create the correct light for the painting of the frescoes the wash was soon scratched through with dozens of cartoons including many of wombats. These last became a specialism of Burne-Jones.

Val Prinsep recalled the atmosphere in the Union while the work was going on:

> But when I paid my first visit there, and for several months after, the inside of the hall was a mass of scaffold, and the whole building rang with chaff and laughter. The favourite animal of Rossetti and his friends was the wombat [sic].

Caricatures of this creature in every imaginable position in all the windows. "Do you know the wambat at the Zoo?" said Rossetti; "a delightful creature – a most comical little beast." I made the acquaintance of this quadruped later, in company with Rossetti himself, who prodded the beast with his stick, and roared with laughter at his movements.

One strange echo of this wombat craze is the Oxford Union's rule 50: 'Any Member introducing or causing a dog to be introduced into the Society's premises shall be liable to a fine of £5. Any animal leading a blind person shall be deemed a cat. Any animal entering on police business shall be deemed a wombat.'

Meanwhile, Morris was discovering two things. The first was that a commitment to medievalism and life as an artist did not make painting frescoes any easier. His part of the figurative painting became increasingly distorted and the butt of Rossetti's always cruel humour, but he then turned to the decoration of the ceiling and, with the help of Charles Faulkner (who would later be one of the founding partners of the enterprise that became Morris & Co.) produced a magnificent bestiary that included not only the serpents, crocodiles and hippopotami known to the medieval world but also, apparently, opossums and wombats. A satirical pamphlet of the time described it thus:

Here gleams the dragon in the air, there roams along a dancing bear; here crocodiles in scaly coats make love to birds with purple throats; and there in vests of brightest green rhinoceroses large are seen; while winking with their weather eye, roll round red hippopotami...

Ruskin thought the design 'clever but not right'. Lady Pauline Trevelyan, who would subsequently become an important patron of the Pre-Raphaelite idea and of William Bell Scott in particular, pronounced it ugly. Ugly or beautiful Morris's original work was lost in 1875 when the Union Committee decided that their hall required a slightly less dazzling carapace. They called in Morris again and the magnificent design to be seen on the ceiling today is the result of the Morris and Co. makeover that the committee commissioned.

The second discovery was Jane Burden, a working-class 'stunner' whose extraordinary beauty must have contrasted strikingly with the ogress to which Morris was devoting his time at the Union. Exhibiting all the lovely innocence of a certain kind of well-to-do young man of the time, he fell in love. And reader, he married her.

So, long before the Top's arrival the Rossetti world was rich in wombats. So much so in fact that, by 1864, Rossetti's sensible brother William Michael was writing from Paris and describing the wombats that he saw there. And not just any wombats: he was able to distinguish between the common and the broad-fronted (*latifrons*) species:

> To the Société d'Acclimatisation. I am glad to find a wombat among the acclimatising animals – a young (I think the common one), not at present blind… Also a full-grown broad-fronted wombat seems in very good condition.

Like Gabriel, William was besotted by these engaging creatures and, as late as 1897 when he spent a brief period in Australia with his daughter Helen, who had gone there in the hope that the climate would help the worrying signs of possible tuberculosis that she was exhibiting, he was keen to bring home a wombat.

ROSSETTI'S MENAGERIE

IN 1862 ROSSETTI'S WIFE, ELIZABETH SIDDAL, DIED. THE TALE of his subsequent grief and eventual breakdown is well known although, as will become clear, his relationship with Top suggests that all was not unmitigated glumness. The effect of this as far as Top's fate is concerned was that Rossetti could no longer bear to stay in the marital home where Lizzie's ghost still walked. George Price Boyce, the minor Pre-Raphaelite

© Tate Images

Illustration 18
   Max Beerbohm's version of Rossetti's garden: the creature snarling at William Bell Scott in the foreground is a wombat

Illustrations 19, 20 and 21
Exterior and interior views of Rossetti's
bungalow at Birchington-on-Sea: by no
means a modest residence

who accompanied Rossetti to see the wombat in 1859, was not worried by this and took the premises over immediately in the much the same way that the sculptor Alfred Gilbert took over the J. P. Seddon designed bungalow at Birchington-on-Sea where Rossetti spent his last days and where he died.

So Rossetti took out a lease on 16, Cheyne Walk. This was a large villa known as both Tudor House and Queen's House and having, crucially for a would-be zoo-keeper, a big garden of some four-fifths of an acre. The house subsequently became the residence of Mrs Mary Eliza Haweis the author of, among other things, *Beautiful Houses* (1882) – a rather quirky study of artist's residences – and *The Art of Housekeeping* (1889) in which she describes Tudor House as 'a handsome little old house, well-seasoned and capable of adaptation to modern needs with little outlay'. More recently the house was owned by the philanthropist and Rossetti collector Sir Paul Getty.

The move to Tudor House (which did not, by the way, still Lizzie's ghost although Rossetti's addiction to drugs and ouija boards would not have helped his state of mind in that regard) opened up the opportunity for Rossetti to indulge his love of exotic animals. He could have indulged his love of beasts and his interest in spiritualism at the same time had he known that one of the ghosts which are said to stalk Cheyne Walk is that of a bear. In fact this area of Chelsea is a hot spot for ursine emanations. At least three different spectral bears have also been seen in nearby Glebe Place. I can take stories of chain-clinking monks and headless women with equanimity but the thought of a ghostly bear trying to make sense of things, or whatever ghosts do, fills me with pity.

In 1862 Tudor House was about one hundred and fifty years old and part of the Cadogan Estate. At first Rossetti lived here with his brother William, Algernon Swinburne and George Meredith. Meredith soon left. Some accounts say that it was on the very first day after he had witnessed the appalling sight of Rossetti at breakfast at which 'he devoured like an ogre five poached eggs that had bled to death on five slabs of bacon' and did not wish to repeat the experience. Others have Rossetti challenging

Illustration 22
Tudor House in the late nineteenth century
(with bay window and gateposts)

Meredith to repeat a remark at which he had taken offence, at pain of having a cup of tea thrown at him. As anyone who has ever read *Felix Holt* will know, Meredith was never one to save words and so the tannic tide broke over him. These are good stories but, towards the end of his life Meredith attempted to set the record straight claiming that he was only concerned by Rossetti's single-minded devotion to his work to the detriment of his health and diet. Later in his life Rossetti was actually put on the modish low-carbohydrate Banting diet by his doctor John Marshall so Meredith was probably right to be concerned about the long-term effects of his youthful eating habits.

Swinburne stayed a bit longer, although in this case, the departure was more to do with chronic inability to pay the rent than with any discomfort, real or alleged, with the company.

William also left but stayed at Cheyne Walk most Mondays, Tuesdays and Fridays. With a large house in his sole possession, Rossetti set about populating the garden with his 'beasts' some of which roamed free (often with disastrous consequences) others of which were penned in (with varying success). He also populated it with his friends and set up a large marquee decked with Persian rugs in which they would on occasion dine while the animals snuffled round them. This marquee seems not to have been a permanent feature. It can be seen in the well-known sequence of images of Jane Morris commissioned by Rossetti from the photographer J. R. Parsons in early 1865. It was re-erected in May or June 1868 when Rossetti hosted a

Illustration 23
Jane Morris in the garden at Cheyne Walk

party in response to William Morris's dinner to celebrate the completion of *The Earthly Paradise* (I suspect that this is the occasion recorded by George Price Boyce in his diary for 1st June 1868). It is not apparent in other images of Rossetti's garden but one assumes that it was not unusual for it to be *in situ*.

Rossetti was not a popular neighbour (as will be seen further below) and the anonymous author of *A Book with Seven Seals*, a memoir of Chelsea life in the 1860s, recalls her Nurse's view of him:

> In Nurse's opinion he was only fit to be a bat and come out in the dusk, flitting up the Walk and in again to hide away from the sun in his great big house, where he painted pictures and kept a lot of poets and other wild beasts, so she had been told... 'She wasn't going to have the children frightened by the likes of him,' Nurse declared, and when she saw him coming she would turn up a side street.

One can get a sense of how disturbing Rossetti's progress may have been from a passage in the diary of his friend William Allingham (author of the once much-read poem *The Faeries* and husband, in later life, of the celebrated artist Helen Allingham):

> Rossetti walks very characteristically, with a peculiar lounging gait, often trailing the point of his umbrella on the ground, but still obstinately pushing on and making way, he humming the while with closed teeth, in the intervals of talk, not a tune or anything like one but what sounds like a *sotto voce* note of defiance to the Universe

That might just frighten the children.

He kept, at various times, all manner of creatures. One was a white Brahmin bull, or zebu (a specimen of the distinctive humped cattle of India). This was purchased on a whim from a 'beast show' in Cremorne Gardens which Rossetti and his brother saw on a visit there in 1864. Rossetti frequently went to this place of entertainment and haunt of prostitutes both to see the various street shows and on the off chance of finding a new 'stunner' – from 1862 onwards you could even telegraph

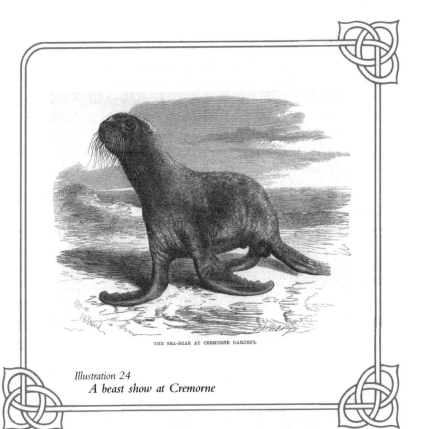

THE SEA-BEAR AT CREMORNE GARDENS.

Illustration 24
A beast show at Cremorne

ahead to book seats in one of the best booths. Phoebus Levin's painting *The Dancing Platform at Cremorne Gardens* was produced in the same year that Rossetti met the bull and thus offers an intriguing visual record of the scene. It shows, pretty much in the centre of the image, some decidedly 'gay' (in the Victorian sense of sexually liberated) women being entertained by a monkey riding on a poodle. Further back there is another monkey riding what looks like a bull terrier. This very entertainment must have been a high spot as it is picked out in William Thomas Moncrieff's 'comic medley song' *The New London Exhibitions* (1850):

> If light is your heart at the end of the day
> To the Gardens of Cremorne by steam haste away –
> Where Quadrilles you may dance, gin and water may quaff,
> And have at the Monkeys and Dogs a good laugh.

Nicholson's 1000 Guinea Fete promised for the nights of 31st July – 2nd August 1843 that ' Mr Alexander Burke's celebrated Poney 'Bobby' will trot seven miles and a half in 30 minutes, with a Monkey on his Back, attired *à la* Chifney, in Jockey Cap, Top Boots and Spurs, and carrying a Whip in his hand.' An advertisement for *The Fete for the Million* held on 29th July 1861 announces a performance of 'Mr Henry Cooke's celebrated Circus Troupe of Educated Dogs and Monkeys.'

The importance of Cremorne as a place of resort for people who wanted a good time can also be seen from the advertisement prominently displayed on the side of an omnibus in Walter Greaves's astonishingly modern image *Hammersmith Bridge on Boat Race Day* (c.1870) which brashly states 'CREMORNE WILL OPEN IN MAY'. Cremorne is also celebrated in racy poems such as William Thomas's *The Chelsea Steamers! Or a Trip to Cremorne* (1850) and James Robertson

Illustration 25
A typical scene at Cremorne

Planché's *Polly Connor* (1881). Both Thackeray and Trollope mention it as a 'fast' entertainment. It was at Cremorne (possibly, and possibly in 1857) that Rossetti met Fanny Cornforth, his long-time model, companion and mistress, who was apparently cracking nuts with her teeth and attracted his attention by throwing the shells at him. This not entirely flattering story appears to derive from Rossetti's friend William Bell Scott. Fanny had another version which is recounted below.

The zebu cost £20. Rossetti paid this sum in instalments, with William being pressed into stumping up the first fiver. This stocky and irritable little creature – Ellen Terry is supposed to have cattily remarked that Rossetti only bought it because its eyes reminded him of Janey Morris's – had to be trussed up and carried through Tudor House which, by this time, was heavily stocked with Rossetti's valuable collection of blue china. It was then released into the garden and this it proceeded to destroy until it was tied to a tree. Unfortunately, the tree was not up to the job and when Rossetti took Whistler to see the bull – Whistler christened it 'a bull of Bashan' – it uprooted its tethering post and pursued him round the garden until the tree finally caught in something and brought this interesting *corrida* to a bloodless end while Rossetti bolted up the garden steps and into the house. According to Whistler (whose stories about Rossetti can rarely, if ever, be trusted) Rossetti called his man (who went by the name of Pope) to capture the bull but this man 'who had gone about the house with peacocks and other creatures under his arm, rescued armadillos, captured monkeys from the tops of chimneys, struck when it came to tying up a Bull of Bashan on the rampage, and gave a month's warning'. But the bull was trussed up again and carried through the house, no doubt casting longing looks at Rossetti's pots, to be given away.

Whistler was later to take out a celebrated libel suit – 'What a lark!' commented Rossetti – against Ruskin for his defamatory criticism of the painting *Nocturne in Black and Gold: The Falling Rocket*. This brought a number of key people in the Rossetti circle together in court and ironically, the painting shows a

Illustration 26
Rossetti in the garden at Cheyne Walk

firework bursting above Cremorne Gardens where they had often met in happier circumstances and not only to buy zebus. Whistler was actually quite obsessed with Cremorne as a subject and also produced, among others, *Nocturne in Black and Gold: The Fire Wheel, Cremorne Gardens No 2, Nocturne: Cremorne Gardens No 3* and *Nocturne in Blue and Silver: Cremorne Lights.* His *Nocturne in Blue and Gold: Old Battersea Bridge* also shows the Cremorne fireworks bursting across the river and this enables us to know exactly the moment that Whistler was trying capture. It must have been between 10.00 and 10.30

Illustration 27
Rossetti and his family in the gardens at Cheyne
Walk showing the steps up which he escaped from
the bull. Left to right: Rossetti, Christina Rossetti,
Mrs Rossetti and William Michael Rossetti

p.m. as that was when Mr Wells, the chief pyrotechnician at Cremorne, set off the nightly display. It was the frankness of the evidence at the libel trial and the clear implication that Cremorne was a place of sexual pleasure that got it closed down. When it finally went, *The Daily Telegraph* of 6th October 1877 sagely commented: 'that the cause of public morality will benefit in the slightest from the disappearance of these gardens would be too ridiculous to suppose' and noted that Cremorne 'was but a poor, struggling, feeble little show from the beginning'.

In Theodore Watts-Dunton's novel *Aylwin* (1898) the painter D'Arcy (known as Haroun-al-Raschid because he never walks the streets except at night) is an amusing and affectionate portrait of Rossetti which starts with the zebu:

> Next morning, after I had finished my solitary breakfast, I asked the servant if Mr D'Arcy had yet risen. On being told that he had not, I went downstairs into the studio where I had spent the previous evening. After examining the pictures on the walls and the easels, I walked to the window and looked out at the garden. It was large, and so neglected and untrimmed as to be a veritable wilderness. While I was marvelling why it should have been left in this state, I saw the eyes of some animal staring at me from the distance, and was soon astonished to see that they belonged to a little Indian bull. My curiosity induced me to go into the garden and look at the creature. He seemed rather threatening at first, but after a while allowed me to go up to him and stroke him. Then I left the Indian bull and explored this extraordinary domain... Soon I came across an object which, at first, seemed a little mass of black and white oats moving along, but I presently discovered it to be a hedgehog. It was so tame that it did not curl up as I approached it, but allowed me, though with some show of nervousness, to stroke its pretty little black snout. As I walked about the garden, I found it was populated with several kinds of animals such are never seen except in menageries or in the Zoological Gardens. Wombats, kangaroos and the like, formed a kind of happy family.

The phrase 'happy family' is a reference to a popular street entertainment by which various animals of supposed natural enmity (such as cats, mice and dogs) were kept together in a cage – there was one almost permanently outside the National Gallery more or less where, in modern times, the ice cream and burger vans used to park during the summer (the satirical pamphlet previously cited described William Morris's ceiling in the Oxford Union as a 'happy family'). Although this passage and others in this novel are obviously fictional they do give a lively sense of what Cheyne Walk felt like when the menagerie was *in situ*. The only other really full description of the garden (apart from an account of the birds that Rossetti kept there in George Price Boyce's diary for 27th October 1866) is from Hall Caine's *Recollections of Rossetti* (1882) which was written as a

THE HAPPY FAMILY

Illustration 28
A 'Happy Family'

memoir of the last years of the artist's life after the glory days of the menagerie had long passed. It was Watts-Dunton who took on the responsibility of looking after Swinburne after he had declined into an alcohol-fuelled incapacity so he had some idea of managing difficult creatures himself. Can it really be true that Swinburne would slide down the banisters naked just for the pleasure of having Watts-Dunton pull the splinters from his mangled buttocks?

Illustration 29
Henry (Harry) Dunn's watercolour of Rossetti
and Watts-Dunton at Cheyne Walk

This bull provoked an echo long after Rossetti's death when an entirely different story was told by Ethel de Pearsall Smith in a letter published in *The Times* of 12th May 1928:

> Readers of Sir Johnston Forbes-Robertson's charming tribute to his friend Dante Gabriel Rossetti will perhaps be interested to know that it was not only the armadillo that escaped in the garden at Cheyne-walk. I have often heard my father tell how the bull broke loose from the tree to which it was tethered, and Rossetti, who was sitting on a stool painting it, fled, head foremost, through the (closed) French window. The animal, a fine young Norfolk bull had been procured for Rossetti by my grandfather, William Haughton Clabburn, of Sunnyhill, Thorpe, near Norwich who was a friend of Rossetti in the painter's early and struggling days.

Now the story of the zebu and the visit to Cremorne Gardens with William is pretty well attested so what is this story about? It is unlikely that the writer is completely fabricating the tale. I suspect that what is happening here is a conflation of two different Rossetti-and-bull stories.

The first is the tale of the 'Bull of Bashan' which she would almost certainly have heard from her father who when still a 'young subaltern' would go to Cheyne Walk with Frederick Sandys 'where he delighted in the sparkling talk'. This talk might well have included Rossetti's telling the zebu story against himself.

The second is the tale of the (unfinished after being commissioned by three different patrons at different times) painting *Found*. This painting, important in the Rossetti canon as a unique foray into modern social realism, includes a white calf. The painting of this calf was a great trial as Rossetti took forever to get it down and the calf kept growing. I suspect that this calf was the 'young Norfolk bull' and it may well have had a practice charge at Rossetti while he was attempting to paint it. 'As for the calf,' Rossetti recorded, 'he kicks and fights all the time he is tied up, which is five or six hours daily, and the view of life induced appears to be so melancholy that he punctually attempts suicide at half-past-three daily PM.' But this particular creature was never part of the Cheyne Walk menagerie: Rossetti painted him in the garden of Ford Madox Brown's house in Finchley (then rural) and overstayed his welcome. His host may also have been nervous about the calf as he would have remembered the devastation wreaked on his flower beds when he also used his garden to paint *The Pretty Baa Lambs* from life.

All this creates another mystery, as Rossetti seems actually to have got the calf from nearby Manor Farm, which is nowhere near adjacent to Norwich. Fanny Cornforth was the model for the 'fallen woman' 'found' by a young farmer modelled by Rossetti's butcher's boy. Another story (Fanny's own) about Rossetti's finding Fanny is that he bumped into her and sent her blonde hair falling irresistibly down her back. In this account the meeting was not in Cremorne but in the Surrey Pleasure Gardens or, in another variant, the Strand (and probably in 1856). But wherever and however Dante met Fanny he had to paint her, just as he had to have the zebu.

By May 1870 Rossetti had acquired two kangaroos – an adult female with a male joey in her pouch. These came to a bad but mysterious end. According to William Rossetti the baby kangaroo was killed by his mother some time in June 1871. But Harry Dunn, who actually lived in Cheyne Walk at the time as Rossetti's studio assistant, said that it was the son who proved matricidal – although this seems unlikely as it could not have been more than two years old at the time of the alleged incident. The surviving kangaroo (mother or son) was still alive as late as 23rd October 1871 when William mentions it in his diary but, according to Dunn, it was subsequently murdered by a vengeful racoon.

Rossetti's racoon was nothing but trouble and Rossetti had to pay compensation for its raids on neighbouring gardens where henhouses in particular proved irresistible. The racoon lived in a box with an Italian marble top but this did not prevent it from vandalising the neighbouring gardens and stealing all the eggs for miles around – sometimes, it has been alleged, burgling houses via the chimneys. Dunn first met the racoon when it was living in this box and Rossetti:

...put his hand in quickly, seized the 'coon' by the scruff of the neck, hauled it out, and held it up, in a plunging, kicking, teeth-showing state for me to look at, remarking 'Does it not look like a devil?

The most scary feature was its eerie crying which the nervy Rossetti feared, as late as 2nd March 1872, might be the keening ghost of Lizzie Siddal. William, being of a more down-to-earth nature, pointed out that it was the racoon that Rossetti had absent-mindedly shut in a drawer. Harry Dunn tells the same story but substitutes Rossetti's long-suffering housekeeper who thought that it was the ghost of her recently dead husband. The racoon disappeared for a time, going missing on

16th August 1870. But according to William, Dante Gabriel did not regret this as 'it used to lie *perdu* and was dangerous to other animals.' However, the racoon was like a recurrent bad dream and came back at least twice more: once to murder the surviving kangaroo (if Harry Dunn's memory served him right) and again to hide in a drawer terrifying both master and servants. It also ate a considerable number of Rossetti's poems in manuscript. This damage was verified much later by his niece Helen who mentioned some correspondence with Holman Hunt, the crucial parts of which had vanished due to the depredations of a rodent. It could have been a mouse of course, there were plenty of them scuttling around Cheyne Walk. Allingham noted that when he staying with Rossetti in October 1867 he sat up late with Harry Dunn and Charles Howell; Howell and Dunn went downstairs to get something to eat from the kitchen and, on their return, Howell reported that he had seen a mouse eating a haddock – but we all know it was the *revenant* racoon.

There were several peacocks. One of these, a glorious white specimen, dived under Rossetti's sofa where it put up such a fight against all comers that it could not be retrieved until after it had died. 'The lovely creature won't respond to me,' said Rossetti. 'No wonder!' said a friend, dragging it out, 'It's dead!' Another peacock was so appalled and outraged when a fallow deer – which itself died in October 1871 – trod on its tail that its screaming caused a neighbourhood furore which still echoes today: the leases of Cadogan Estate houses explicitly prohibit the keeping of peacocks. It must be said though that the noise must have been very great, as the deer was so startled by the peacock's display that it fell into the habit of stalking it and stamping on its tail until, bit by bit, all its feathers were out. This nuisance (and indeed, the nuisance caused by the many henhouses in Cheyne Walk) was the subject of a letter to *The Times* of 18th August 1869:

> In conclusion [the writer has hitherto been complaining about the noise made variously by bargees and revivalist preachers] I must tell you that everybody here, of course, keeps poultry, and a bantam on my right hand, whenever he chooses to do it, is

sufficient in his small treble to wake up and irritate all the hoarser cadences of full-size cocks who defy him, while, at the same time, not merely 'ever and anon' but always, we have to endure the cackling provocations of some hen, varied by an interjectional scream celebrating some event which no one cares to understand but themselves.

That last comment must surely refer to Rossetti's peacock and the noise even moved Carlyle, whose studies were constantly disturbed by the bedlam, to one of his grisly jokes: 'I have no objection to their hatching, if they would only do it in peace and leave me to do the same.' Notice also the corroboration that there really were rich pickings for an ovomaniac racoon.

Surprisingly, the Estate does not also ban armadillos as some of Rossetti's set up mining operations into the neighbouring gardens and, apparently, drove a sap into the kitchen of Tudor House itself. 'If it isn't the devil, there's no knowing what it is,' said the cook, no doubt just before handing in her notice. In 1928 Sir Johnston-Forbes Robertson remembered an armadillo incident:

> One day he [i.e. Rossetti] brought an armadillo into the studio to show me. The creature escaped from his arms and darted under a piece of furniture. Down on his knees went Rossetti, hauled the animal out, and turned it over that I might admire the colour of its corrugated pink stomach.

The armadillos would also rush into neighbouring gardens at top speed, their advent heralded by the dreadful tearing sound made by the privet hedge as it gave way before their armoured assault. Rossetti's put-upon neighbours were, on one side, Edward Cooper and his wife, the manager of a commercial concern and, on the other, Mrs Georgania [sic] Stuart, a widow, and her three unmarried daughters. Their 1881 census return shows that they lived on 'Income from Interest of Money'.

Things got so bad, and Rossetti's garden so perilously full of holes, that by 24th April 1871 he had steeled himself to do away with the armadillos forever and provided them with a meal of a chicken (this is William's account, Harry Dunn says it was chopped beef) laced with prussic acid. This they seem to have consumed with no ill effects except, perhaps, to the blood pressure of Rossetti's neighbours as four days later renewed evidence of digging showed that the poison had been nothing but a tonic to them although they were no longer to be seen scuttling around. On 23rd October 1871 William thankfully noted that they had disappeared 'and are supposed to have burrowed into some neighbour's premises'. 'They are said to have been very destructive to pigeons etc', he added. And who knows what damage lurks in the 'etc'? The racoon also seemed to have thrived on prussic acid so perhaps Rossetti's growing tolerance for strong chemicals was being transferred to his non-human companions. Probably the worst noises came from the owls and the laughing jackass (Australian kingfisher) – ordered from the exotic animal dealer Jamrach together with a marmot and some other creatures on 5th November 1867 – that would cause Harry Dunn to start from sleep trembling whenever it set off its weird shriek.

There was a horde of dormice, some of whom Rossetti gave as presents to William Morris's children in late April 1868, plucking them from his pockets as he stepped through the door. He had owned a dormouse as his first childhood pet (the creature's name was Dwanging) and probably remembered his care in peeping at it while it hibernated and his glee when it woke up in the spring. Perhaps it was purchased from one of the Savoyard hurdy-gurdy men who were a distinctive street presence in mid-nineteenth-century London and kept mice, marmots and squirrels in cages which rotated as they played. You can see one of them in William Powell Frith's painting *Ramsgate Sands: Life at the Seaside* (1854) which was purchased by Queen Victoria and kept at Osborne House. So he well knew what pleasure he could give the children by such a present. In his adult years he threw a party to celebrate the awakening of his dormice (whom he provided with little bamboo chairs, presumably this was an exercise in Aesthetic *Japonisme*) from their winter sleep but in spite of his prodding them and exhorting them to wake up, they were all dead.

He wrote the children a lovely letter that is worth quoting in full:

> Dear Jenny and May,
>
> Here come 2 little dormice to live with you – I know you will take great care of them and always give them everything they are fond of – that is nuts, apples, and hard biscuits. If you love them very much I dare say they will get much bigger and fatter and remind you of Papa and me.

This is an interesting example of two things. Firstly, Rossetti's tendency to find parallels between his menagerie and his human circle; secondly, the kindness which is such a feature of contemporary accounts and a quality which runs against much else that one reads about him. His normal practice with regard to his animals was to love them while they enthralled him and then neglect to care for them until they died or had to be given away to 'good homes'. In spite of the warmth of affection that Rossetti inspired in his friends and their consequent readiness to forgive what seems with hindsight his sometimes appallingly selfish behaviour, it often feels that they suffered from the same up-and-down intimacies and that he lavished on his beasts. On 5th May 1868 a letter to Jane Morris gives us a depressing picture of life as a dormouse in Cheyne Walk:

> I am very glad little Jenny and May liked the dormice... What do you think? Yesterday the stray dormouse was caught at last. I had heard a scratching constantly in the room for a day or two, but never guessed what it was or thought of looking in the trap till yesterday afternoon, when I found the poor little chap in it almost dead, hardly thicker than his tail and with his eyes nearly shut but still gnawing at the wires...

Why didn't he think to look in the trap? And, by the way, this letter comes at a time when Rossetti and Janey's complex love affair was beginning to come to the boil. As William recalled, 'several of these animals came to a bad end... the dormice would fight and kill each other, or would eat up their own tails, and gradually perish'. There seem also to have been cats in the household although none are mentioned in any contemporary source that I have found. Helen Rossetti later remembered that her uncle was very fond of cats and had 'his own peculiar way of fondling them and folding them up'. Which sounds ominous.

There would have been an elephant too. Rossetti told Robert Browning that he felt that it would be a good advertisement as he would teach the creature to clean the windows:

> Then when someone passes by the house he will see the elephant cleaning the windows, and will say, "Who lives in that house?" and people will tell him, "Oh, that's a painter called Rossetti", and he will say, "I should like to buy one of that man's pictures". So he will ring and come in and I shall sell him a picture.

This story was confirmed by Ethel de Pearsall Smith who retold her father's memory of Rossetti's frustration with the difficulty of getting a reliable window cleaner and his vow to 'go round to Jamrach's and get a dam' elephant'.

But if Rossetti was only seeking such a creature to make a sensation and advertise his presence – though the peacocks, armadillos and racoon seem to have done that pretty successfully – he did go as far as enquiring the animal dealer Jamrach's price. This proved to be £400 for a small African specimen and this was steep even for a man so well supplied with 'tin' as Rossetti – he would have had to have sold a painting to his long suffering patron George Rae. Of course, he did eventually acquire 'a good old elephant' in the form of his companion and eventual nurse, the model-prostitute Fanny Cornforth (née Sarah Cox) whose great size in later life caused Rossetti to make the unflattering if affectionate comparison. He produced several cartoons of Fanny as an elephant: in 1873 he drew an elephant swimming and entitled it 'Dear old Fan'.

Later there was a woodchuck with which Turgenev played affectionately when he dined at Cheyne Walk on 23rd June 1871. Rossetti loved the woodchuck and William recorded how he would play with him in the same way that he would play with Top:

He would sit with either [i.e. wombat or woodchuck] in his arms by the half-hour together, dandling them paunch upward, scratching gently at their cheeks or noses, or making the woodchuck's head and hind paws meet. With the wombat no such operation was possible.

Illustration 30
Rossetti's woodchuck

A drawing by William Bell Scott shows the woodchuck on Rossetti's lap and very nice it looks too. Scott thought that it was a wombat and wrote as much on the back of the paper which meant that when the drawing was put up for sale on the second day of the posthumous auction of Rossetti's possessions (6th July 1882) it was described as 'Lot 829 A pencil sketch of Wombat' but William Rossetti later corrected the error. One does wonder, however, if the drawing said to be of a dormouse which is to be found on the back of the sketch for Rossetti's *King René's Honeymoon* in the Birmingham City Art Gallery is actually an image of a wombat. It certainly looks like one and, if so, is the only drawing of a wombat produced by Rossetti himself apart from the two cartoons reproduced elsewhere in this book – the date, alas, is too early for it to be a picture of Top.

G. P. Boyce also recalled a whist and supper party at Cheyne Walk with the woodchuck (he called it a marmot) wandering around the dining room floor. Rossetti had 'called for it' like Old King Cole.

There might have been a lion but Rossetti was put off by the expense of running hot water pipes through the garden to keep him warm in winter. He probably got this idea from the Royal Menagerie in the Tower where some sort of heating was, in the last days of that facility's existence, provided for the lions.

Rossetti had many other animals: there was Punch the Pomeranian, Wolf the Irish deerhound (who languished from lack of exercise and had to be given away), Jessie and Bobby the barn owls. Bobby sounds an enchanting creature: Christina described it as 'a little owl with a very large face and a beak of a sort of eggshell green'. There were wood owls and Virginian owls, one of whom lost a claw when Rossetti tried to remove it from its box on 5th November 1867, the second of whom died some time in mid 1870. These seem to have been pretty lively. William Allingham recorded a visit to Rossetti on 15th October 1867 and noted the 'fierce Virginian owls which dash against the bars of their cage to get at you as you turn away'. There were also Chinese horned owls. The love of owls, like the

Illustration 31
Dormouse or wombat?

love of wombats, appears to have run in the Rossetti blood. William's daughter Helen kept an owl and you can see it in Herbert Gilchrist's 1894 portrait of her father – it is sitting in a wicker cage on the study floor staring up from one orange eye and looking not unlike a Persian cat who is harbouring a minor grudge. In her diary Olive Garnett recalled seeing this as a work in progress on a visit to William's house and actually referred to it as 'Mr. Gilchrist's portrait of W. M. R. and the owl's cage'. There were all sorts of mice, squirrels, rabbits and hedgehogs (who must have lived a nerve-racking life with all those owls about), parakeets, chameleons, lizards, salamanders, more woodchucks, marmots and a solitary mole. This last kept, presumably, to make sure that not a shred of decent lawn would sully the prospects of Cheyne Walk.

There might even have been a penguin. Rossetti was negotiating for one in late 1871 but thought the £10 price too steep and was trying to enlist William to throw in £3. This, the ever faithful brother appears to have been prepared to do, in spite of his no doubt correct belief that 'the penguin, living in so unnatural a condition, will die almost as soon as it is bought'. Thankfully for all concerned the penguin was sold, probably to Antwerp Zoo, on 5th December.

There was a cunning old grey parrot whose best trick was to entice a visitor to pet it and then try to take his or her finger off. The parrot had been taught, perhaps by the servants, to say 'You ought to be in church now' when it heard the bells of nearby St Luke's church. Rossetti or his servants had missed a trick here as Cezanne's parrot apparently used to squawk 'Cezanne is a great painter' and what a come-on for would-be patrons that would have been, almost as good as a window-cleaning elephant. It had also been taught other things it seems and used to keep Rossetti and Jane Morris amused on her unchaperoned visits to model at Cheyne Walk in 1868, when her relationship with Rossetti was beginning to fill both their lives. It fell out with a neighbouring parrot owned by George and Mary West and attacked it. George was a tailor and made clothes for, among others, the Pre-Raphaelites. He also fitted out Thomas Carlyle whom the parrot had somehow learned to insult by making a noise like the tapping of a stick and crying 'There goes old Carlyle!' So Rossetti was not the only keeper of nuisance animals in that part of Chelsea.

JAMRACH AND OTHER MENAGERISTS

AND THEN THERE WAS TOP, ONE OF TWO WOMBATS, THE SECOND of whom died almost immediately and about whom little is recorded beyond its purchase on 14th May 1870 and its prompt demise on 26th of the same month.

Top came into a glorious menagerie. Into a prosperous Bohemian household where ghosts jostled with racoons, and antique Persian carpets with the latest fashion in fabrics on Rossetti's lady sitters; where prostitutes became virgins and poisons became medicines. One tale that neatly sums up the chaotic atmosphere is that Top ate a lady's hat. She was the cherishably named Mrs Emily Virtue Tebbs, the wife of Rossetti's patron and solicitor Henry Virtue Tebbs, and known to Rossetti as 'merry Emily'. Rossetti's only reaction was to fear for the wombat's digestion. This may well be a true story as although Rossetti's crayon portrait of Mrs Tebbs is usually dated to 1870 it is by no means unlikely that she was visiting Cheyne Walk in late 1869 for preliminary sketches or consultations. Unfortunately, although the sketch was still known to be in Mrs Tebbs's possession in 1899 there seems to be no record of its present location. Indeed, it probably no longer exists.

But Top's life started before Cheyne Walk and we should now trace his origins if not as far as Australia then certainly into darkest London and the impoverished streets of the East End.

Charles Jamrach was internationally famous as were his immediate descendants. There was a Jamrach dynasty and it is not always easy in looking at the various stories that surround them to tell which Jamrach is being referred to. You can still see the grave of the first Charles Jamrach (he died in 1858) and his wife Mary in Tower Hamlets cemetery. Charles Jamrach junior

died on 6th September 1891 at the age of 76 and was sufficiently distinguished to warrant a comic obituary in *Punch*. The last important animal-dealing Jamrach was Albert who was Charles's son and he died in 1917. Albert largely concentrated on birds, perhaps because as he got older his father's trade in boa constrictors ('very brisk' according to *The Times*) started to get too much for him. But if you wanted an animal, Jamrach was your man.

The founding fathers of the Berlin Zoo sought his help and advice in the acquisition of rare animals as, previously, Carl Hagenbeck, the founder of Hamburg Zoo, had bought up the Jamrach patriarch Gotthold's 'Handels Menagerie', to start his collection in 1863. Rudyard Kipling, Andrew Lang, E. V. Lucas and H. G. Wells all mentioned Jamrach in their books.

Even Barnum consulted him. According to Mark Twain it was Jamrach who acted as Barnum's agent in buying Jumbo (on a

Illustration 32
Animals for Jamrach's shop being unloaded in London

shopping spree that included among its must-haves, Shakespeare's birth-place, Madame Tussaud's Wax Works and the recently captured King Cetewayo of Zululand). It is certainly true that Barnum did attempt to purchase these monuments and tried to get hold of Cetewayo and that he finally did pick up Jumbo – there was a national outcry and questions in Parliament – but I am not sure whether Jamrach really was his agent or whether this is another fine example of Twain's irrepressible humour and love of a good spoof. What is interesting though is that Twain plainly expected his readers to know who he was talking about and this is surely a sign of Jamrach's international reputation. In Saki's tale *Reginald's Drama* the protagonist speculates happily on the sensation that will be made by the programme note 'Wolves in the first act by Jamrach'. In *Dracula* the wolf Bersicker that escapes in the frenzy caused by the Count's malign influence is noted as coming from Jamrach's, and one has to speculate that Bram Stoker hit on this provenance for his lupine character after a talk with Rossetti. Stoker also lived in Cheyne Walk and it may even be that he got the idea for Lucy Westenra's *post-mortem* perambulations from his near neighbour's exhumation of Elizabeth Siddal. It is certainly possible. Late in his life Jamrach himself ventured into print with an article in the *Boy's Own Paper* (1st February 1879) describing his fight with a tiger that had escaped from his shop (see below). Jamrach was particularly known for exotic birds – cockatoos, parrots, macaws – many of which made their first entry into the country through Jamrach's shop and sometimes sold at prices which are high even by today's standards and not allowing for any change in the value of money. Jamrach is supposed to have imported the first ever budgerigars to be seen in this country and, having bought a pair for £26, sold them to a Dr Butler of Woolwich for £27. Richard Bell, who made a very extensive collection of animals over his life and recorded them in his memoir *My Strange Pets* (1905), noted that he bought a pair of emus from Jamrach for £20.

The shop was one of the sights of the East End. American tourists visited it and the carriage trade patronised it. One of

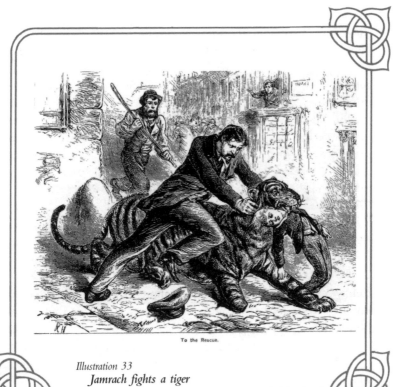

To the Rescue.

Illustration 33
Jamrach fights a tiger

the photographs of it that I have been able to find dates, I would say, from the early twentieth century and shows a rather unassuming premises next door to Harris's and Lipman's (which looks like a drapers from the window display). Jamrach's appears to be double-fronted (plenty of room for elephants) but there is no sense of the remarkable, and the people lounging around in front of it are more interested in the photographer than in the contents of Jamrach's windows – which must have been surprising although I suppose that if you lived in that neck of the woods, passing kangaroos and wombats every day made them no more interesting than a pile of apples or potatoes. The street is not prosperous but not all of the Jamrach family lived there. For example, William Jamrach, who wrote to *The Times* about tapirs in 1878, resided at a somewhat more gentlemanly address: 6, Somerset Villas, Lordship-road, Stoke Newington.

Illustration 34
Jamrach's shop

But in 1901 George Jamrach, another son of Charles, was still living in St Georges Street (Ratcliff Highway was so renamed to try to still the memory of the notorious Ratcliff Highway murders of 1811 – the suspected murderer, who committed suicide before trial was and, presumably, still is buried with a stake through his heart at the intersection of New Road and Cannon Street) where his father had first set up home having seen the vast number of ships in the port of London, especially St Katherine's Docks, and realising that he could emulate his own father's trade but on an even grander scale. I have also seen one report that places a Jamrach depot in Liverpool but I have been entirely unable to track this down although it makes good sense and at least one other wild animal dealer, William Cross, who was Jamrach's main rival in the trade, had premises in Liverpool. There was certainly some kind of menagerie in the basement of what is now the Liverpool branch of John Lewis's before the Second World War.

Illustration 35
An advertisement for Cross

In 1877 an anonymous American contributor to *Harper's New Monthly Magazine* described a visit to Jamrach's. The shop was set on the Ratcliff Highway where 'the police never dream of suppressing vice and villainy... being only too glad if they can give it a semblance of outward decorum... this they can do at any time other than Saturday evening'. Various accounts of Victorian London (Watts Phillips, *The Wild Tribes of London* (1855), Charles Dickens (Jr), *Dickens Dictionary of London* (1879), Montague Williams, *Round London: Down East Up West* (1894), for example) all describe Ratcliff Highway as an area of unspeakable debauchery, lawlessness and violence. The only bright hope comes from Donald Shaw (writing as 'One of the Old Brigade') in his *London in the Sixties* (1908). Shaw trots out the usual stuff and then turns to Jamrach's shop:

> Continuing along St George's Street will be found Jamrach's menagerie, whence filter most of the rarities that find their way into the Zoological Gardens; and the place is no ordinary bird shop, but a museum of information in more ways than one. Here one large room will be found stuffed with bronzes and curios from all parts of the world, which every American visiting London, who fancies he is a critic, does not fail to inspect; for Mr Jamrach – like his father – is an authority, and a naturalist in the highest acceptation of the term.....Lovers of animals will not regret a pilgrimage to 'the Highway' which, by the aid of the District Railway and broad, electric-lighted streets, in so no longer attended with discomfort or danger.

As late as 1946, Sir Garrard Tyrwhitt-Drake remembered, in *The English Circus and Fairground*, an 1891 visit to Jamrach's (under the management of Albert) with great clarity and affection, and noted that by that time the Ratcliff Highway had lost some of its fierce reputation. In the 1860s, however, Rossetti had no fear when it came to buying animals or curios and for a connoisseur of working-class stunners, a trip down east would have had other benefits too.

But poor Top! What a start for a genteel wombat and we can see him grieving in his cage while the bottles flew outside. And if the population of Jamrach's was much the same in 1869 as it was in 1877 Top would have shared his lodgings with marmosets, boa constrictors, cobras, frogs, terrapins, tortoises, thousands of birds (packed from floor to ceiling in a room of 'death-like stillness' where 'not one little heart was cheery enough to chirp' – as the writer of the *Harper's New Monthly Magazine* article sadly observed), three small elephants, a black bear (to be sold as a pet – kindliness guaranteed – and Jamrach to be personally liable for any baby he may hug to death) a crane, several baboons and monkeys, seals, emus, Tasmanian devils, cats, ichneumons, racoons, two tigers (for the imperial gardens in Constantinople, £420 to the Sultan himself) and a lion (about to go to a Rajah in India for £100). The Honourable Harold Finch-Hatton recalled meeting Big Ben, a massive crocodile (twenty-three and a half feet long) in Australia and then seeing him again in Jamrach's shop.

A couple of years earlier, the Reverend Harry Jones (who fought the good fight in the dives of East London) reflected, in his memoir *East and West London* (1875), on what a stroke of luck he enjoyed to serve in the only parish where 'a parson could ring his bell and send his servant round the corner to buy a lion'. From the Rev. Jones we learn that Jamrach's shop mainly stocked birds and that the larger mammals were kept in a yard in Betts Street. He also tells us that Jamrach did not advertise but rather announced the arrival of new animals with a regal notice in the papers of London, Paris, Berlin, and Vienna. Jamrach was so confident in his pre-eminence that his announcements gave his address solely as 'Jamrach's'. If Rossetti's menagerie caused havoc in the relatively genteel reaches of Chelsea, Jamrach's occasionally added to the mayhem on the Ratcliff Highway. George Sims recalled a herd of Icelandic ponies peaceably taking the air in Prince's Square (to his credit William Morris let his Icelandic pony Mouse live out his life munching the rich green grass of Kelmscott rather than sell him to Jamrach) but Harry Jones tells us of the day a tiger escaped, picked up a boy by the collar and padded off to a quiet corner in order to eat him. An attempt to mount a rescue by attacking the tiger with a crowbar succeeded – in some accounts – only in killing the boy (the tiger ducked). Jamrach himself finally managed to secure him. According to Harry Dunn this event happened only a few days before he visited Jamrach's with Rossetti ('with time to spare and being so close to Jamrach's establishment it occurred to Rossetti that ere returning home he would look in there and buy something in the bird or animal line') and Jamrach himself beat the tiger back into its cage with a crowbar. So the common features of the two versions are a tiger and a crowbar but according to Dunn, Rossetti bespoke a 'Wambat' and this is interesting because, if true, this wombat would have arrived at Cheyne Walk in 1867 (it is possible to date this visit on other evidence which will be alluded to below) two years before Top and, otherwise, entirely unrecorded.

Other sources date the tiger incident to 1857 which suggests that Dunn heard the story on his visit to Jamrach's ten years later but didn't realise it referred to a far from recent event. In fact the incident happened on 26th October 1857 when a tiger escaped from its cage and picked up a boy called John Wade, severely injuring him. Jamrach drove the tiger back into its cage by hitting it with a crowbar breaking its nose and little John was carried off to hospital where he was expected to die. Newspaper accounts of the time vary as to whether Jamrach aggravated John's injuries by striking him with the crowbar. The story was widely reported throughout Britain, even making the Welsh language newspaper *Baner Cymru*. By 29th October the *Daily News* reported that John Wade was now making a recovery. *Punch* found the whole thing a hoot and *The Examiner* of 31st October published a skit entitled 'A Poor Dear Tiger' in which it accused Jamrach of not paying enough attention to the rights of the tiger (in favour of the boy) and making a comparison between this event and the war against the mutinous sepoys then raging in India (with the clear and astonishingly modern implication that too much attention was being given to the sepoys' rights and welfare). However, public interest in the story did not end there as a week later Jamrach sold the tiger, broken nose and all, to Wombwell's menagerie for £400.

The tiger was plainly of an exceptionally lively disposition: no sooner had he arrived at Wombwell's – where he was, somewhat irresponsibly, advertised as 'the tiger that swallowed the boy' – than he broke out of his cage again and then into that of a peaceable lion who lived next door, giving him a fearful mauling mitigated only by the lion's thick mane which, literally, saved his skin. The story finally came to an end on 5th February 1858 when, in the case of Wade vs. Jamrach, a jury awarded the young Wade £60 in damages (£50 more than the £10 Jamrach had lodged with the court) for his injuries which, although largely healed, had left him with a nervous predisposition and a tendency to bite his brother. In the *Boy's Own Paper* article mentioned above Jamrach claimed that the judge showed much sympathy for him, saying that although the law bound him to award damages he felt that Jamrach ought to be rewarded rather than punished. Stories tended to stick to Rossetti: even in a case like this – which is very well documented in the Victorian press – subsequent commentators on Rossetti's life have tended to prefer the more colourful versions of events. As if the truth were not colourful enough.

Amazingly, this was not the first time a tiger had been on the loose in the Ratcliff Highway. One escaped from Wombell's

Illustration 36
Sceloglaux albifacies

menagerie in January 1839 and *The Morning Chronicle* described its progress through the East End. This creature ate a dog and lacerated anyone who got too near, but was eventually recaptured.

There is also a story about a bear escaping from Jamrach's. This animal was eventually found in the company of two little girls who were prudently feeding him honey. There are memorials depicting both this event and the escape of the tiger in Tobacco Dock. But it is still possible to see an animal that actually lived in Jamrach's shop. The Zoological Museum of Amsterdam has a specimen of the now extinct Laughing Owl (*Sceloglaux albifacies*), a New Zealand bird that had no defence against imported cats.

This was purchased from Albert Jamrach on 6th July 1881 for the large sum of fifteen pounds but died, in spite of being in a specialist zoological facility, on 16th January 1882. A stuffed white cougar now in the Rothschild Museum at Tring (once the site of Walter, 2nd Baron Rothschild's significant and marvellous menagerie where cassowaries roamed the grounds together with the zebra that, from time to time, were harnessed to Rothschild's carriage: he took thirty kiwis with him when he went up to begin his undergraduate career at Cambridge) may also be the one that lived in London Zoo between 1848 and 1852, having been bought from Jamrach, but the provenance is more doubtful.

What both Jones and other commentators also remind us is that, in addition to his stock of wild animals, Jamrach had a considerable repository of curios and antiquarian goods from the orient, the Pacific and Africa. Presumably sailors who had slipped in to convert their parrot or baby alligator into beer money also unloaded their carved tusk or samurai sword. This makes good sense as Gotthold Jamrach, Charles's father was originally harbour master of Hamburg and began the trade by casually buying oriental and other exotic curiosities, both living and dead, from the crews of the ships that docked there. Evidence for this is a shrunken head in the Pitt Rivers museum in Oxford which, according to the catalogue, was bought from

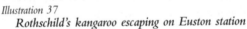

Illustration 37
Rothschild's kangaroo escaping on Euston station

Jamrach by Pitt Rivers himself in 1874. Jones notes that, as a result of the antiquities end of the business, many wealthy people (such as Rivers and Rossetti) visited Ratcliff Highway and one wonders if it was Rossetti's enthusiasm for eastern antiquities – which is well attested by the catalogue of his possessions auctioned after his death – and particularly Chinese blue porcelain, that first led him to this Cockney forerunner of Liberty and Co., the shop of choice for the various arts movements of the time. (Liberty opened in 1875 with, as one of its chief attractions, a large oriental department which drew on the experience of its founder Arthur Lasenby Liberty as manager of Farmer and Rogers' Oriental Warehouse.)

One wonders, for example, if the 'Curiously carved mahogany frame chair with cane seat formerly belonging to the Chinese giant Chang' (sold off after Rossetti's death) was a purchase from Jamrach or if Rossetti picked it up on one of his forays to Cremorne or a similar pleasure ground. Chang was 6' 9" tall and a well-known figure in Britain after his arrival from China in 1864. Curiously, he brings together a number of the themes in this book as he toured with Barnum and also visited Australia. After this exciting life he died in 1890 as the proprietor of a tea shop in Bournemouth.

In Dunn's memoir, Rossetti was in the region of Jamrach's when the tiger escaped, because he wanted to include a Nubian in the water-colour *The Return of Tibullus to Delia* (1867, but first sketched out as early as 1852) and so he had gone to the Sailor's Home in Whitechapel where he thought he would find just the thing. And so he did, but when the boy turned up in Cheyne Walk next day he was so dark that Rossetti said you could see his clothes moving but not the boy. I do wonder however whether Dunn was confusing this event with another. It was very probably on another shopping trip to Jamrach's that Rossetti had noticed a little black boy sobbing his heart out on the steps of a hotel. The boy was an American slave (though legally he was free as soon as he set foot on English soil) travelling with his owner. Now, this suited Rossetti very well as he was at that point developing a picture for his Liverpool patrons George and Julia Rae. This was to become *The Beloved* and originally the plan was include a Negro girl (later depicted as a mulatto) as the cupbearer. But when Rossetti saw the boy, this scheme went out of the window and the boy became as desirable as the armadillo or Qing vase that he had been on his way to buy. So back they went to Cheyne Walk to paint the boy, the boy crying all the while. Rossetti pointed out – and there is an almost querulous tone here one feels – that the boy's tears made his skin even darker where they had streaked down his face. Rossetti's maternal aunt Charlotte (being less aesthetically motivated, and thus able to tell the difference between art and life) later thought that the boy was crying for his 'Mammy'. But the picture was eventually completed and sold for three hundred pounds – in typical Rossetti fashion it fell way behind schedule and Rae was persuaded to pay one hundred guineas as a down payment on another painting (to cost eventually four hundred guineas) in order to encourage Rossetti to finish the original commission. But whatever Rossetti's views on slavery and race (quite ambivalent one would have to say at least when compared with the naked racism of Whistler which looks nasty, even making allowance for its time), the painting is one of the very few portraits of an Afro-American in a state of slavery. As it was started in 1863 and largely completed by 1865 – when Dunn joined Rossetti's establishment – it is also, almost certainly, the last. All because of Rossetti's collection and menagerie.

★★★

The wealthy visited Jamrach to buy all sorts of animals. But they also visited to sell them. Lord Baden-Powell recorded, in his *Lessons from the Varsity of Life* (1933), that on his return from India he sold his pet panther Squirks to Jamrach. Baden-Powell had tried to give Squirks away but no one would have him for more than twenty-four hours as he was 'so strong and mischievous'. Baden-Powell also drew some charming cartoons of Squirks, one in the act of leaping over a table and destroying, in the process, a vase and a flower arrangement – he would have fitted into Cheyne Walk only too well. Jamrach also bought a famous lion from a travelling menagerie: this animal was called Nelson and Jamrach eventually gave him to the zoo where he lived until 1872. Some of Jamrach's patrons were serious collectors. One such was the nature writer Eliza Brightwen who lived at The Grove in Stanmore, Middlesex. She kept two home museums. One was of minerals, anatomical specimens and rare seeds. The other was a dead zoo and came, in part at least, from Jamrach. In 1890 she obtained an Indian gazelle which, in spite of living in the conservatory, died of cold. She also bought an Egyptian lizard (whom she christened

Rameses): this couldn't have fared much better as it ended up in a glass case. A flamingo stood stuffed and far from its home on the Nile while above hung the preserved corpse of Impey the bat – also purchased from Jamrach. Eliza documented one of her visits to Jamrach's shop. On this occasion she bought Rameses the lizard, a tortoise, and two Peruvian guinea-pigs with 'eyes just like boot buttons'.

Among the general madness of the shop she was shown some armadillos and these, like the hedgehogs in *Alice in Wonderland*, rolled themselves into balls – the connections between Top, Rossetti, Jamrach and Alice will surface again later in the story. The ancestors of these creatures no doubt had spent their lives busily undermining the foundations of Rossetti's Cheyne Walk neighbours. It is an insight into the animal trade at this time that Jamrach advised that, should Eliza buy the armadillos and become bored with them, they would make an excellent dinner. She also mentions a yard where larger animals, including a camel and a kangaroo-rat, lived. Whether this was the Betts Street depot described by Harry Jones is not clear.

Eliza was to leave better records of her household's non-human complement than Rossetti left of his and in her books *Wild Nature Won by Kindness*, *Inmates of my House and Garden*, *More on Wild Nature*, *Quiet Hours with Nature*, and *Last Hours with Nature*, she documented no less than fifty-two different animals, each of them named. As this record does not include such luminaries as Rameses we must assume she had many more creatures than she ever had time to write about. Her menagerie was, however, different from that compiled by Rossetti. It was a mixture of what we would now call 'rescue animals' such as Dick the starling, Asnapper the owl, or Sylvia the wood-mouse as well as exotica purchased from Jamrach or other dealers such as Impey the bat, Spectre and Phantom the lemurs or Tommy and Perlie. The first of these was a ruffed lemur purchased from a travelling zoo, the second a ring-tailed specimen purchased from Bedford Conservatories in Covent Garden. Lastly there were exotica sent (how?) by relatives throughout the Empire and beyond. These included Birdie the Virginian nightingale,

Cheops the scarab beetle, Mungo the mongoose and Sancho the Second, the Italian toad.

What Eliza's collection represents is a halfway house between modern notions of keeping animals as pets, companions (as represented, for example, by the significant collection maintained by the young Beatrix Potter in her nursery at Bolton Gardens) or as a philanthropic gesture, and traditional Victorian (and earlier) notions of the conservatory as *Wunderkammer*. Her collection brings together traditions of organic naturalism and the beginnings of modern environmental consciousness with another idea about animals. This is that they are the spoils of (colonial) war and another way of imposing the appearance of ownership over the ends of the earth. Rossetti, on the other hand, was a straightforward collector although there can be no doubt as to the pleasure he got from his motley of pets. His menagerie also had something that Eliza Brightwen's did not: it had a wombat.

Rossetti's was not the only private menagerie in London. Up in Highgate, Baroness Angela Burdett-Coutts was keeping llamas on her lawn and she must have got these from Jamrach. She may also have had emus. In Knightsbridge the novelist Charles Reade also had a fair collection. A painting by Charles Mercier shows him with Puff, a white spitz, and when the subsequently famous lawyer Sir Robert Anderson lodged in Reade's house as a young man he was much pestered by the dog. Reade was horrified and, as Anderson recalled in his memoir *The Lighter Side of my Official Life* (1910), advised that should it happen again he should 'entice him into your room and leather him.'

Another of Jamrach's customers was Frank Buckland. He was the son of William Buckland the Dean of Christ Church (Oxford), the ground-breaking palaeontologist who more or less single-handedly laid the foundations of modern knowledge about dinosaurs. Dean Buckland was a keen naturalist but his naturalism took a strange form as he determined to eat his way through the animal kingdom. He ate all manner of insects and slimy things. He wondered whether bluebottles or moles tasted worse. Reputedly he took a bite from the embalmed heart of

Louis XIV when he was shown it out of its reliquary at Nuneham Abbey and when shown a supposed martyr's blood, miraculously liquefied on a cathedral floor, he dipped his finger in it and pronounced it to be nothing more extraordinary than bat's urine. Ruskin wrote that he regretted missing a tea of mice on toast when he was invited to the Buckland household. (Another keen mouse on toast eater of the time was the eccentric campaigning journalist William Stead who, apparently, got the idea from reading about the privations endured by Parisians during the siege of 1870. Stead was author of the sensational article on child prostitution *The Maiden Tribute of Modern Babylon*, and was last seen reading a book in the first class smoking room of the *Titanic* as the ship went down.)

On one occasion, dinner was interrupted by a terrible crunching sound coming from beneath a *chaise*: it proved to be a hyena munching a guinea pig and this was perhaps appropriate as it was Buckland's discovery of the pre-historic hyenas' den at Kirkdale Cavern in Yorkshire in 1821 that made his reputation. In 1822 Buckland's friend William Conybeare published an amusing cartoon showing Buckland entering the cavern and being confronted by a party of live hyenas and one wonders if this was inspired by Conybeare's knowledge of Buckland's domestic arrangements. Dean Buckland was also a strict disciplinarian and when a monkey turned up drunk at Christ Church he had it escorted off the premises.

Frank followed in his father's footsteps and in one of his early undergraduate conversations rattled his new friends when he complained that earwigs were so 'horribly bitter'. You'll be interested to know that the boiled head of an old porpoise tastes like 'broiled lamp wick' – but how would you know that unless you had eaten a broiled lamp wick? As a child he had ridden a near-dead crocodile that his father had placed in the pond in Christ Church quad in order to revive it. But in adulthood he kept a bear known as Tiglath-Pileser (Tig) who attended various Oxford functions dressed in cap and gown. It is apt that such an erudite bear should have been given such a name as Tiglath-Pileser, who was King of Assyria from 1115 to

1077 B. C., and is the first person whom we know to have founded a library.

The little bear met many famous people including Florence Nightingale and Richard Monckton Milnes who hypnotised Tig at a garden party in the Oxford Botanic Gardens. Florence Nightingale was no stranger to animal mesmerism – she mesmerised her pet owl Athena (which can still be seen, stuffed, in the Florence Nightingale museum) in order to coax it into a cage when she first acquired it. It is said that Tig also rode a horse and drank champagne. (In this he was like Sir Thomas Stanford Raffles's pet sun bear who would often join him for mangoes and bubbly after dinner; Raffles's private zoo unfortunately perished in a shipwreck on its way back to England in 1824 but when Raffles himself got home he founded London Zoo as if to make up for his loss.) But one day Tig escaped and terrified the village of Islip by stealing all the sugar from the local shop. Frank had little option but to give him to the zoo. After Tig's death Frank had the bear stuffed.

Frank was especially keen to extend the range of animals as foodstuffs. His father was more of an experimental gourmet but Frank went at it much more systematically, requiring a cut of any creature that died at London Zoo. He sampled a leopard that had been two weeks dead and buried before Frank found out about it and ordered it exhumed from the flower bed in which it had been deposited. Through the offices of the Society for the Acclimatization of Animals, Frank organised dinners at which various exotic beasts including *holothurian echinoderm* (sea slug) and kangaroo were served. In order to get people interested in eating horses he organised an all-horse banquet for 160 people but admitted to himself that horsemeat would never attract the British even if it was disguised by the name 'hippocreas'. He did nearly succeeded in naturalising the eland and a number of aristocrats including Viscount Hill, the Marquis of Breadalbane and Lord Egerton set up herds on their estates. Frank also thought, probably correctly, that the kangaroo would thrive but was not convinced that people would ever learn to eat it – although when William Morris once found himself on his own at Kelmscott Manor, having neglected to tell the servants he was coming, all he could find to cook was a tin of kangaroo meat.

But it was fish that really caught Frank's interest. In this he may have been following his father's neighbour Anna Thynne's example (this was when William was made Dean of Westminster). Anna invented the aquarium and conducted fundamental research into marine life in her drawing room using glass tanks and barrels of sea water brought up the Thames each day and aerated by hand. But Frank was especially keen on fish farming and fly-fishing with which he enthused the Prince of Wales. His greatest achievement was probably the stocking of Australia and New Zealand with trout (salmon did not do so well), the eggs being shipped over from the great trout streams of England packed in ice. Frank Buckland was a friend of Jamrach and this mention of Australia now brings me back to Top.

-TOP-
A WOMBAT ABOUT CHELSEA

ALL DESCRIPTIONS OF JAMRACH'S SHOP HAVE TWO THINGS IN common: awe at the sheer spectacle of so many birds and animals crammed in together and melancholy at the obvious desperation or dejection of so much of his stock. So when a gentleman came and paid Jamrach £8 for receipt of one wombat it must have seemed to Top that things were looking up. Wombats were plainly in demand as Jamrach advised that if the price was a problem there were plenty of gentlemen who were ready to pay it. But a man who earned over £3,000 per annum and who would pay £20 for a demented Bull of Bashan was not going to blench at £8 for a wombat. Top was expensive: only eleven years before, the magazine *Leisure Hour* noted that Jamrach's price for a kangaroo was fifty shillings (£2.50). This doesn't sound very much but wombats were much rarer than kangaroos.

So Top came to Chelsea at last. Unfortunately, Rossetti himself was not at Tudor House to greet the new arrival. He had retired to Penkill Castle in Scotland to nurse his imaginary eye troubles (he suffered from a hypochondriacal belief that he was going blind) and to try to get some relief for his insomnia. William Bell Scott recorded that during his stay here Rossetti contemplated suicide by throwing himself from the cliff overhanging the pool known as the Devil's Punch Bowl. But all was not hopeless gloom and when you read Rossetti's letters of the time you can see that one of the reasons he could not sleep was his happy anticipation of the coming of the wombat. He first mentions Top in a letter to Jane Morris dated 11th September. 'What do you think?' he asks, 'I have got a wombat at Chelsea'. His studio assistant, Harry Dunn, who had actually collected Top from Jamrach's, thoughtfully supplied him with some sketches and these so enchanted Rossetti that he sent them to Janey together with a poetic postscript:

> Oh! How the family affections combat
> Within the heart, and each hour flings a bomb at
> My burning soul; neither from owl nor bat
> Can peace be gained till I have clasped my wombat!

So Top was both a sedative and a cordial. It must be said, however, that Rossetti's own recognition of the stimulant qualities of late night owl screeches might have given him a clue as to the root of his sleeplessness, given the number of those birds that he kept roosting at Cheyne Walk. On 14th September a very detailed letter to William setting out amendments to the volume of poetry that Gabriel had in train ended 'Have you seen the Wombat?'

His sister Christina sent him an Italian poem:

> O Uommibatto,
> Agil, giocondo,
> Che ti sei fatto
> Liscio e rotondo!
> Deh no fuggire
> Qual vagabondo
> Non disparire
> Forando il mondo
> Peso davero
> D'un emisfero
> Non lieve il pondo.

(O wombat, agile, joyful, how have you grown, furry and round! Ah do not flee like a vagabond, do not vanish, burrowing through the world: it's really the weight of a hemisphere, not a light burden.)

William annotated this poem somewhat prosaically in his edition of Christina's verse:

Christina took it upon herself to Italianize this form of the name of the *Wombat*, which was a cherished animal of our brother. It will be understood that she is exhorting the Wombat not to follow (which he was much inclined to do) his inborn propensity for burrowing, and not turn up in the Antipodes, his native Australia. As a motto to these verses Christina wrote an English distich:- When wombats do inspire, / I strike my disused lyre.

Rossetti thanked Christina for this poem in a letter to William of 15th September. In this correspondence he refers to 'the shrine in the Italian taste that she has reared for the Wombat', adding 'I fear his habits tend inveterately to drain architecture'. This reference to a shrine is usually taken to refer to the *Uuommibatto* poem. But I have never been entirely clear as to why this should be so. I would rather think that she had built Top a kind of kennel. Was the slab of Italian marble that was lying about in Rossetti's garden when he was trying to control his racoon three years later a piece of architectural salvage from this short-lived structure?

In the same letter he declares that he has got some instructions as to feeding the wombat from Nettleship 'who is always at the zoo'. This was John Trivett Nettleship, an early admirer of Blake – as was Rossetti – who frequented the zoo to follow his vocation as a fashionable painter of wild animals not as a naturalist, so one wonders just how suitable his dietary regime actually was. The always reliable William dropped round to Tudor House on 18th September to check that all was in order before Gabriel's return home and this is when we get our first real view of Top whom he described as:

> ...the most lumpish and incapable of wombats, with an air of baby object-lessness – not much more than half grown probably. He is much addicted to following one about the room, and nestling up against one, and nibbling one's calves or trowsers.

And William, you will recall, really knew his wombats. In his later reminiscences of his brother he recalled that 'no more engagingly lumpish quadruped than the first wombat could be found'. Tantalisingly one of William's letters tells a slightly different story:

> The wombat, whom I saw yesterday, is the greatest lark you can imagine: possibly the best of wombats I have seen. She (for

I believe it is a she) is but very little past babyhood, and of a less wiry surface than the adult wombat: very familiar, following one's footsteps about the room, and trotting after one if one quickens pace – and fond of nestling up into any hollow of arms or legs and nibbling one's trousers

But at no other time is Top ever referred to as 'she'. William may have been wrong of course: he had seen more wombats than most Englishmen who had never left western Europe but if the creature was very young it might have been no mean task to tell what sex it was. If Top really was little more than a baby when s/he came to Cheyne Walk that does, of course, make his/her connection with the Duke of Edinburgh less likely, although the difficulty of getting wombats to breed in captivity makes it highly improbable that Top was born at Jamrach's. Disentangling truth from fiction and fact from legend is not easy in this case and Top remains, in certain respects, an enigma.

On 20th September Rossetti finally got back to London and next day set to writing to his Penkill friends Miss Losh and Miss Boyd. Miss Losh was the first recipient of a detailed account of Top's appearance and habits:

> I have seen no one as yet except the parrot and the Wombat who are on either side of me as I write – the former letting fall a remark – or shall I say an animadversion ? – from time to time – and the latter burrowed deep in the sofa cushions indulging apparently in the more abstruse forms of thought. He is a round furry ball with a head something between a bear and a guinea-pig, no legs, human feet with heels like anybody else, and no tail. Of course, I shall call him 'Top'. His habits are most endearing. He follows one about everywhere and sidles up and down stairs along the wall with the greatest activity. He is but a babe as yet and very rough as to his coat which however is splendidly thick. The Consummate Wombat is quite smooth, and such he will be when adult. He is tremendously good-natured. I know you would pronounce him a perfect darling.

Later that day he had had some more experience of co-habiting with a wombat and put some more detail into a letter to Alice Boyd:

I have not yet seen anyone but Dunn and the Wombat. The former is meritorious and the latter 'a joy, a triumph, a delight, a madness'. You will love him at first sight. He is a babe at present and rougher in his coat than he will turn out. His habits are of the school of 'Contemplative Absorption' so that W. B. [William Bell Scott] might add a passage on him to *The Year of the World*. However his affections are of the sweetest kind and he follows one about like a dog, and if his leader hastens on, so does the Wombat. I am told he gallops round the garden but have not seen him do so yet.

Still later that same day Gabriel quoted the identical passage from Shelley's *Prometheus Unbound* that he had used in his letter to Miss Boyd when he wrote to William – the choice is interesting as William was, at this time, engaged in editing Shelley's poetry which he had adored for many years. Not one other of Rossetti's animals seems to get the same level of detailed attention and one can agree with his rather hostile biographer Evelyn Waugh that 'it does not appear that Rossetti lavished any personal affection on his various pets, except perhaps upon the first of his wombats'. William remembered that 'Dante's affections were prodigalised [on] the first wombat'.

But by 27th September Nettleship's diet was having its effect and William recorded that Top was already showing signs of 'some malady of the mange kind' and was being attended by 'a dog-doctor'. I suspect that this may well have been the sarcoptic mange to which Joséphine's wombat fell prey and this is certainly the most likely illness. This might confirm that Top came from Tasmania or Flinders Island where the mange is endemic in the wombat colonies; other Australian wombat pop- ulations are less prone to it. Sarcoptic mange would also explain the 'objectlessness' and passivity that characterise accounts of Top. On the other hand it is a very disfiguring condition – one can still see the skin of Joséphine's wombat, complete with mange, in the Muséum nationale d'Histoire naturelle – and one which is transferable to human beings in the form of scabies so one has to wonder if Top would have appeared so sweet if he was really suffering from full-blown sarcoptic mange. He could equally well have picked up some other parasite – perhaps from a dog or one of the rabbits with whom Dunn's early sketches for Rossetti show Top as being housed.

Next day Top had rallied and was well enough to meet Ruskin and burrow between his coat and waistcoat while he expounded his views on the necessities of communal organisation. This is an interesting encounter as it is often cited in asides about Rossetti and in previous sketches of the life of Top. I would love to think it was true but, although Ruskin and Rossetti still knew each other and occasionally met, their relationship had been pretty cool since 1866. The source is Rossetti himself:

> Ruskin called the other day and seemed to tend towards a grand proposal of banding together for the regeneration of the world. I told him that any individual I came near was sure to be the worse for it. You should have seen him wring his hand and soul towards his forlorn species, while the wombat burrowed between his coat and waistcoat.

Ruskin's diary for the relevant period has no mention of any visit to Cheyne Walk and certainly no mention of having a wombat (especially a mangy wombat) crawling under his coat. Ruskin was a strange man but I think that even he might have mentioned such an event especially as he was fond of animals himself and, throughout his life, owned a series of dogs. Tim Hilton's remarkably comprehensive biography of Ruskin doesn't mention this incident. It's another wombat conundrum.

Things looked bleak again on 28th September when William, no doubt thinking of the blind wombat that he and Christina had seen in Regent's Park a decade earlier noted that Top 'shows already decided signs of the loss of sight that afflicts so many wombats.' This is, of course, not necessarily a sign of disease but a feature of all wombats as their mainly nocturnal habit does not require keen eyesight and the lateral placement of the eyes does not facilitate forward vision. But it is ironic, as Rossetti had gone to Penkill to try to alleviate the physical strain and emotional turmoil caused by a real or imagined deterioration in his own vision.

During his brief life Top used to dine with the artistic and literary elite of Victorian Bohemia. Rossetti would place him in a very tall silver épergne on the table of his first-floor drawing room (which he used as a dining room when entertaining) and there he would slumber while talk of art and politics and, one assumes, sex and money, flowed round him. Whistler claimed that on one such occasion Top used the distraction of a row between Meredith and Rossetti – no doubt they were trying to drown out Swinburne's vigorous intonation of *Leaves of Grass* – to clamber down from his argent perch and consume a box of cigars. But given that Whistler claimed that Top died as a result of this escapade, and we know the circumstances of his death fairly accurately, this is likely to be a good story rather than a true one. Perhaps Joseph Knight's version of the story is more realistic:

> The wombat used to sleep on the épergne in the middle of the dinner table, entirely indifferent to the talk, the movement and the lights. On one occasion it took advantage of a particularly enthusiastic and absorbed discussion to descend from its place and gnaw the contents of a box of expensive cigars.

It is quite possible that a curious wombat, no doubt keen to supplement an inappropriate diet, may have experimented with chewing tobacco. It is probably from this story, as retold by Ford Madox Brown, that the idea has developed that Top was the model for the dormouse in *Alice in Wonderland*. This is certainly a nice thought but it cannot be correct, as the relevant parts of *Alice* were written by 1864 and thus well before Top was in residence. However, Lewis Carroll was a visitor to Cheyne Walk in 1863 and took a number of photographs of Rossetti and his family in the garden where Top was to live. Is it possible that he did conceive the idea of a menagerie *cum* tea party on one of these visits? It isn't that difficult to see Rossetti as the Mad Hatter and he did have a lot of dormice. The only thing that leaves a chink open for the story to be true is the mention of the 'wambat' ordered by Rossetti in Dunn's account of the visit to Jamrach's that possibly took place in 1863 (assuming Harry Dunn's memory was very faulty). The weight of evidence is that it is no more than a fable but you never know with Rossetti and wombats. In 1859 Mrs Gaskell noted, in a letter to Charles Norton, that Rossetti was 'not as mad as a March hare but hair-mad'. Her attempts to have a conversation with him were constantly thwarted by his habit of rushing off to be introduced to any woman he saw who had red curly hair. So there is a curious and oblique link to the world of *Alice in Wonderland* after all. The épergne, judging by Dunn's watercolour of the dining room, may well have been the 'very handsome plated centre stand' sold as Lot 400 of the Rossetti auction.

On 6th November Top died. William described his death as coming 'after some spasmodic symptoms' and saw it as 'one more instance of the extraordinary ill-luck that has attended Gabriel's animals'. He added that he did not 'assume that my brother wept over them' [i.e. Top and the woodchuck which replaced Top in his affections] but certainly 'his heart was sair'. On 26th November Boyce visited Rossetti and found him 'in a morbid and rather depressed state'. Rossetti sketched himself in deep mourning and penned a parody of the beginning of 'The Fire Worshippers' from Tom Moore's once popular poem *Lallah Rookh* by way of Top's epitaph:

> I never reared a young wombat
> To glad me with his pin-hole eye
> But when he most was sweet and fat
> And tail-less, he was sure to die!

As we have seen, Top's replacement died more or less immediately but the wombat-like marmots and woodchucks that succeeded him were rather more robust. Tantalisingly William recorded Top's eventual fate in his diary entry for 15th December:

> The poor wombat has now been stuffed, and figures in the entrance-hall: his "effect" is not satisfactory.

Ou sont les wombats d'antan? I would dearly love to know if somewhere there stands a little stuffed wombat gathering cobwebs and spilling sawdust.

I never reared a young Wombat
To glad me with his pin-hole eye,
But when he most was sweet & fat
And tail-less, he was sure to die!

Illustration 38
Rossetti lamenting the death of his wombat

-TOP-
THE GO-BETWEEN

THEY DID THINGS DIFFERENTLY IN THE PAST BUT THE astounding thing about all of this was that Top's brief life corresponded with an incident of astonishing intensity and strangeness in Rossetti's life. This was the exhumation of Lizzie Siddal. He chose the enigmatic Charles Augustus Howell to organise this task at which his solicitor Henry Virtue Tebbs (the husband of 'merry Emily') was also present. Howell had been Ruskin's secretary but was sacked in 1870 and Rossetti took him on between 1872 and 1876. Howell (who was remembered as 'the worst man in London' in Conan Doyle's Sherlock Holmes story *The Adventure of Charles Augustus Milverton*) claimed to be a Portuguese nobleman and always wore the red ribbon of the Order of Christ (Morris thought he must have stolen it) but it appears that his father was actually an English merchant. He was full of tall stories and, having heard his performance at the dinner table one evening, Ruskin's mother is said to have remarked in exasperation: 'How can you two sit there and listen to such a pack of lies?' The two were, of course, Ruskin and Rossetti. But he did tell some whoppers: he claimed to have seen a man with a dog's head and excused the extravagant lateness of his arrival for a dinner at the Burne-Jones household by claiming that his hansom cab had crashed into another that proved to contain his Doppelgänger who had handed him his own card. Georgiana sat and fumed. He is officially recorded as having died of pneumonia in 1890 but the story also runs that this was a cover for the fact that he was found in the gutter with his throat slashed and a golden half-sovereign in his mouth. That is the authentic Howell.

He was also a fancier of oriental china and there are many good stories about the rivalry (including stealing from each other's houses) between him and Rossetti for the possession of fine pieces. He was the perfect man to arrange a clandestine exhumation. And, of course, he would have known Top.

Rossetti had sought permission for the exhumation so that the manuscript book of poems he had buried with Lizzie could be retrieved. The publication of this notebook would enable Gabriel both to come before the public as the model of a husband devoted even beyond the grave to his tragic young wife and also to publish, in disguised form, some further poems more recently written and aimed at Jane Morris. These expressed a most improper degree of passion and suggestions of intimacy towards a married woman, particularly a married woman who was the wife of a close friend. Even someone as good-natured and liberal-minded as Morris, who went so far as to move out of his own house to allow Rossetti and Jane the space (as we would say now) to work out their relationship, might have found the public humiliation of such a book hard to bear. Rossetti's relationship with Jane Morris was almost certainly never sexual – for a start Rossetti suffered from a hydrocele (gross swelling of the testicle) which would have limited his sexual capacity and may have made him impotent. It has been suggested that they did consummate the relationship during a brief stay in the feminist painter Barbara Bodichon's cottage at Scalands near Robertsbridge in 1870 but recent research has established that even during this time Jane lived in a separate house. In fact, the time at Scalands was more like a house party and several notable figures in the Rossetti–Morris circle stayed at various times. The most notable event of this holiday was that Rossetti first started taking the chloral that would eventually destroy his stability. He was introduced to it by William Stillman, the American husband of the painter Maria Spartali (who was also staying at Scalands), and for ever after Stillman – who had after all acted in what he genuinely thought were Rossetti's interests – tried to play down his involvement in this incident.

But Rossetti and Jane certainly behaved in a most intimate manner. The designer and ceramicist William de Morgan remembered seeing Rossetti carefully scraping the cream off some strawberries and then solicitously spoon-feeding them to Jane at a dinner party. But at no time did William Morris appear unaware of what was going on – indeed he actually delivered Jane to the house near Robertsbridge and visited her there – and was often included in the private letters in which Rossetti expressed his feelings for Jane. In my opinion, a Burne-Jones cartoon showing Dante Gabriel bearing what are suspiciously priapic cushions in pursuit of a somewhat surprised Jane may show, more eloquently than anything else, the air of sublimated desire (on his part at any rate) that permeated their encounters both public and private. I wonder if this image may not also incorporate a sly dig at the state of Rossetti's genitalia.

Having said all this we should also remember that Morris himself was involved in an intense emotional relationship with Georgiana Burne-Jones. He had first met her while they were still both very young. It was at the Royal Academy in June 1855 and he was looking at Millais's painting *The Rescue*. She was obviously smitten by him and recalled the meeting thus:

> He looked as if he barely saw me. He was very handsome, of an unusual type – the statues of medieval kings often remind me of him – and the drawing of his mouth, which was his most expressive feature, could clearly be seen. His eyes seemed to me to take in rather than give out. His hair waved and curled triumphantly.

Morris was a wealthy young man who was still attempting to find an *entrée* into the art world at this time. He was also, as throughout his life, not socially adept and would have been unable to pursue any interest in Georgiana (who was one of the four highly talented MacDonald sisters – Rudyard Kipling and Stanley Baldwin were her nephews) with any subtlety. Indeed, he would probably have been too shy to go beyond acknowledging her. But a spark obviously passed between them and it almost painful to speculate on what might have happened had they formed any kind of partnership then. (Or not happened – one feels that the extraordinary creativity of Morris and his circle was partly driven by the complexity of the emotional relationships and the sublimation of other interests.) But two years later Morris was in Oxford on Rossetti's 'jovial campaign' at the Union. His meeting with Jane Burden led to their marriage in 1859 (Burne-Jones married Georgiana the next year) and it has been unkindly speculated that Rossetti encouraged this as he saw it as a way of keeping Jane within the circle. He was already too deeply committed to Lizzie Siddal to break off with her in order to take up with Janey. Rossetti's cartoon of Morris giving Jane an engagement ring is not affectionate and reflects an attitude that was to dog their relationship for another quarter of a century.

The relationship between Jane and Rossetti continued to develop throughout 1868 and 1869. In 1868 she was sitting for him in Cheyne Walk and becoming progressively more ill from the mysterious disorder that seems to have affected her for much of her adult life. William, who had now completed his

Illustration 39
The M's at Ems

major poem *The Earthly Paradise*, took her to take the waters at Ems and Rossetti sent her a cruel cartoon entitled *The M's at Ems*. (Even from the early days Rossetti's drawings had a vicious streak, they contrast with the beautifully affectionate images of Morris done when Burne-Jones was in light-hearted mood.) The cartoon shows William declaiming from *The Earthly Paradise* while Janey sits in a bath in the posture used for her depiction in Rossetti's painting *La Pia de' Tolomei*, an image of a woman trapped in a loveless marriage.

Throughout this period Rossetti was writing to both William and Jane in the most intimate terms. It has been suggested that Jane used her illness both to distance herself from the possibility of a sexual relationship with Rossetti and as a way of positioning herself in his affections. I do not believe there was ever a sexual relationship between them although later in life Jane did have a consummated relationship with Wilfred Scawen Blunt, who appears to have seen his position as her lover as a gruesome way of getting closer to his dead idol Rossetti. When Jane and William returned to England Rossetti moved in with Jane and the two Morris daughters at Kelmscott Manor, which he jointly leased with Morris, while William stayed in London. William then left for an extended tour of Iceland in 1871. During the time that Rossetti and Jane were at Kelmscott, Rossetti produced an exquisite portrait of Jane, generally known as *Water Willow*, which I much prefer to some of the many formal images of her he produced. But also during that time something happened, and when William returned from his quest for the sagas Rossetti was gone. I suspect that it was clear that Jane would not leave William and, I think, that in spite of his occasionally monstrous behaviour, Rossetti's respect for Morris prevented him from pressing on with the affair into the realms of public scandal and disgrace. His relationship with Morris was never renewed at its former pitch of intimacy and eventually Janey became an occasional nurse as he sunk into addiction and illness. However, it can be difficult, at a distance fully to understand the nuances of relationships, and certainly the memoirs of Watts-Dunton give a glimpse of Rossetti and Morris together at Kelmscott which gives a far more congenial picture than that painted by most biographers or, indeed, by Morris's own letters.

While all this was going on, Georgiana Burne-Jones was coping with the discovery of her husband's affair with the Greek sculptress Maria Zambaco (née Cassavetti) who had left her husband in 1866, soon after which she took up with Burne-Jones. The more one considers the complexities of the relationships that obtained within this close-knit group, the more understandable Morris's tolerance of Rossetti's pursuit of Janey becomes. John Marshall, the doctor who attended Lizzie Siddal the night she died, whose family were early adopters of aesthetic and arts and crafts style and who was, eventually, a resident of Cheyne Walk himself, was shocked when on visiting what he thought was Burne-Jones's studio, to discover what he felt was a very suspicious arrangement with an adjacent premises occupied by Maria. It is significant that Georgiana did not deal with 1869 in her volume of *Memorials* except through a chapter allusively entitled with a quotation from Keats – 'Heart, thou and I are here, sad and alone!' In January of that year Maria attempted suicide while on a quest for Burne-Jones who was trying to get away from the whole mess by escaping to Rome with William Morris, although he could not bring himself to cross the channel and had an emotional breakdown instead (as indeed he had had while attempting to go on honeymoon).

Rossetti noted all this with a callous glee:

> Poor old Ned's affairs have come to a smash altogether, and he and Topsy, after the most dreadful to-do started for Rome suddenly, leaving the Greek damsel beating up the quarters of all his friends for him, and howling like Cassandra. Georgie has stayed behind. I hear today, however, that Top and Ned got no further than Dover... She provided herself with laudanum for two at least, and insisted on their winding up matters in Lord Holland's Lane. Ned didn't see it, when she tried to drown herself in the water in front of Browning's house etc – bobbies collaring Ned who was rolling with her on the stones to prevent it, and God knows what else.

I find the jaunty reference to a laudanum suicide interesting in one who at this time was supposed to be at the height of his guilt and grief for his late wife whose death by laudanum overdose may well have been suicide (there is an uncorroborated story that Rossetti admitted towards the end of his life that there was a note) and extremely telling of Rossetti's state of mind at this time. There must have been a fair bit of noise as Browning kept geese in his garden (another bad neighbour) and these would undoubtedly have set up an alarm if Rossetti's account is anything like true. The whole event also included Luke Ionides, one of the London Greek family who were such great patrons of the Pre-Raphaelite and Aesthetic Movement artists. He was a would-be suitor to Maria as well and, according to another account, it was he who extracted Maria from the clutches of the bobbies (attempted suicide was a criminal offence at this time). Luke however was irritated and jealous and made no effort to keep the scandalous events a secret. At this time another painter in the Morris–Rossetti circle, John Roddam Stanhope, may also have been Maria's lover, so there was no shortage of opportunities for mischief.

But Burne-Jones and Maria Zambaco still had adjacent studios in remote premises as late as November 1888. Jeannette Marshall (the daughter of Dr John Marshall) recorded this discovery in a tone which hovers between primness and delight at a salacious memory:

> We are rather exercised about Mme Zambaco. When M. and I went to her studio in Campden Hill Road the other afternoon, & found it all shut up, a man offered to ring the bell for us, and while waiting, he volunteered some information. There are only 2 studios side by side, and one is Mme 'Zambago''s (like lumbago!) & the next Mr Burne-Jones', 'Royal artist' added our informant with a flourish. Now knowing that B. J. has a large studio at the Grange, & that Mme Z. did not know we knew of her studio there (wh. P. found out by many enquiries at her former rooms) & remembering the set out there was between them before, it looks very odd! I feel quite disgusted to think that she is going on agn. in the old style. It is a shame! If I were Mrs B. J., I wd. soon have her

wig off! P. actually mentioned the man's remark when he & M. called at Shepherd's Bush to Mme Z., who looked uncomfortable, wh. I don't wonder at. How very inopportune! – I don't like the look of it at all.

Jeannette was fifteen when the great scandal broke so it is interesting that after all these years it should have been so remembered. Most of Burne-Jones's images of Zambaco were produced in 1869 and 1870 including the nude portrait entitled *Venus Epithalamia* which was commissioned, somewhat tactlessly one might think, by Maria's mother in 1870. A stained glass window made by him in 1877 for Lanercost Priory is plainly based on Maria even though it purports to depict St Luke. Was it produced from earlier sketches or from life? There is also evidence that Burne-Jones commissioned Charles Fairfax Murray to produce a secret image of Maria in 1874. The Burne-Jones household finally settled down after all the excitement but I wonder if the price was for Georgiana to turn a blind eye to what became a long-term relationship. And in the last few years of Burne-Jones's life she may well have turned the same blind eye to his relationship with the prominent society hostess May Gaskell, to whom he wrote a sheaf of passionate letters. The complexities of all these comings and goings seem characteristic of the Pre-Raphaelites and, it has been argued, springs from their tendency to use each other as models and to invest the sittings with enormous emotional intensity. Millais fell in love with Ruskin's wife at the very time that he was painting his famous portrait of her husband in Scotland and Henry Wallis ran off with George Meredith's wife while Meredith was sprawled in Wallis's studio pretending to be the dead body of Thomas Chatterton. At Penkill, William Bell Scott lived happily in a three-way relationship involving himself, his wife Letitia Norquoy, and Rossetti's friend and correspondent Alice Boyd.

Georgiana and Morris drew closer together in spite of the latter's flight to Ems in October and, on her birthday in 1870, Morris presented her with an exquisite illuminated manuscript of his own poems (the *Book of Verse*) complete with a little roundel portrait of himself on the front (painted by Charles

Fairfax Murray who had worked for Rossetti and would work for Burne-Jones – Morris had rather taken this promising young man under his wing and treated him to a trip to Bruges for his twenty-first birthday). About the same time Morris had begun experimenting with painting again and the rarely mentioned or reproduced *Aphrodite* (1869 or 1870) is plainly a portrait (though not drawn from life) of Georgiana. It is very possible that many of the poems in the *Book of Verse* were about his own feelings for Georgiana, just as Rossetti's book of the same year was full of longing for Janey, but these feelings were never taken beyond wishes as both he and she were overwhelmingly decent people and bound by ties of love and loyalty to their partners. In addition Morris was concerned with Janey's chronic maladies and, in an act of astonishing magnanimity, he also held that Rossetti too was ill and therefore not fully responsible for his actions. On one manuscript of a poem written at this time he added a candid note to Georgiana: 'Poets' unrealities, tears can come with verse, we two are in the same box and need conceal nothing, don't cast me out – scold me but pardon me.'

Perhaps the most touching evidence of Morris's state of mind at this time may be found in two stanzas of the poem he wrote in a copy of *The Earthly Paradise*, which he gave as a Christmas present in 1870:

> Ah, my dears, indeed
> My wisdom fails me at my need
> To tell why tales that move the earth
> Are seldom of content and mirth.
> Yet think if it may come to this –
> That lives fulfilled of ease and bliss
> Crave not for aught that we can give,
> And scorn the broken lives we lead;
> Unlike to us they pass us by,
> A dying laugh their history.

> ...

These words, never designed for publication and so, we might think, entirely authentic, are a rare insight into William Morris's emotional life. When Rossetti died William thought that there was 'a hole in the world' and Janey said that 'he was not as other men'.

Into this complex world came Top and so did Lizzie's dead body. She was, according to the witnesses, found to be well preserved: a fate Rossetti was also to try to ensure for Top through the taxidermist's art. All this happened in October 1869 when the licence for the exhumation was agreed, and the notebook was finally retrieved from the grave on the fifth of that month. At this point in his life we might have expected Rossetti to be overwhelmed by his guilt (did Lizzie kill herself because she was so unhappy? did he cause her to become a laudanum addict?), grief, and the weight of his complex feelings both for his dead wife and for Janey Morris. There was the strange episode of the near suicide at Penkill and, while there, he became convinced that a chaffinch which landed at his feet and allowed him to pick it up was the spirit of Lizzie. Did the pink of the chaffinch's breast feathers remind him of the pink dove in his portrait of the dead Lizzie, *Beata Beatrix*? After he left for London it was noticed that he, or rather his Doppelgänger, could still be heard pacing about his bedroom at Penkill reciting poetry.

But what was he actually doing in London? Was he grieving over the body of Lizzie (which he never saw as he did not attend the exhumation himself)? He was beginning to worry about the state of the manuscript. Gruesomely there was a large wormhole right through 'Jenny', the poem that he was most keen to have again. He was also concerned that the chemical treatment of the book, which was necessary before he could have it to work on again, might damage it beyond repair. In fact, it did not and some pages still exist. Above all other things he was playing with a fat little wombat and writing comic poems about him. Indeed he seems to have been so distracted that when he wrote to William on 13th October telling him what he had done he said that the exhumation had happened 'on Wednesday or Thursday last, I forget which'. He had decided to save William's feelings by keeping his plans from him and did not attend the exhumation himself although this was also probably because Lizzie had been buried in what was then the Rossetti family grave and so her exhumation would have necessarily involved the disturbance of their father's body.

Now, it may be that he was trying to seem ultra-casual and so play down the importance of the event and, thus, the exclusion of the loyal William from his intimate counsel. It may also be that other events – his love for Janey Morris, his focus on the new poems, the arrival of Top – simply pushed the exhumation of Lizzie down the list of his priorities. Or it may not have been all that important to him. The trouble that Rossetti took to publish his verses may not have seemed worth it in the end as the book stimulated a most hostile review in the form of Robert Buchanan's anonymous attack *The Fleshly School of Poetry*. Rossetti responded himself with a pamphlet on *The Stealthy School of Criticism* and some surprisingly modern attempts to create positive spin by arranging counter reviews from his friends, including a glowing one from Morris published in *The Academy* of 14th May 1870 (at a time, remember, when he had little reason to be fond of Rossetti). Morris's conclusion 'Nor do I know what lyrics of any time are to be called great if we are to deny that title to these' are generous words spoken, even grudgingly, of a man who was pursuing his wife and had, in effect, made it impossible for him to live in his own house. Privately, Morris detested the task and his most sympathetic and tactful biographer Mackail noted that:

> Rossetti's strange fancy of a literary conspiracy against him, and his elaborate attempts to inspire favourable notices of the volume, are matters of common knowledge. Morris, with other friends were dragged into the business; and his article bears all the traces of a task, for once, executed against his will. It is stiff and laboured, and as nearly colourless as anything of his writing well could be.

Ultimately it was the hostility and the critical controversy that created a greater sensation than the poems themselves and so Rossetti's coded message to Janey was somewhat spoiled.

When we consider the nature of Rossetti's life and, particularly, his relationships with William and Jane Morris perhaps his apparent indifference to the exhumation and his infatuation with Top is not so surprising. William's nickname from the early days was Topsy and so Rossetti's choice of the name Top for his wombat was both a reference to Morris's large and lumbering form and, I think, a way of mastering him through the proxy

Illustration 40
Mrs Morris and the wombat

of the wombat. In 1869, while Top was still alive and while the exhumation of Lizzie was in train, he drew a cartoon of Janey (known in the Rossetti–Morris circle as Mrs Top) in true Pre-Raphaelite style, complete with halo. In her left hand she holds a leash, on the end of which is tethered a wombat also with a halo. The shading makes the wombat look as if it has a Morris-like beard. Is this Rossetti's fantasy about Jane's control over William? Is it even a not particularly sublimated wish to see William dead and Janey free? Rossetti had produced cruel fantasies involving Morris's death before – notably the vicious skit *Rupes Topseia* – although he always, in both private and public communications, wrote about his friend and rival's work as both poet and artist in the most respectful terms.

Whatever the truth of the matter it is pretty clear that Top's arrival in Cheyne Walk provided Rossetti not only with a diversion at a time of illness and emotional confusion but also formed another link in the covert chain of signals he was sending out to Janey Morris. He could hide his amorous poems to her in the book plucked, quite literally, from the tangled hair of the dead Lizzie Siddal and he could hide his fantasies about overpowering, mastering and seeing her husband dead in his playful relationship with Top. In naming his wombat Top, Rossetti also reclaimed the relationship that I believe he thought he was to have with Morris back in the 1850s. Top was dependent on Rossetti for everything and when Morris first attached himself to Rossetti in the Pre-Raphaelite days he had everything to learn about art and literature. My sense of Morris's character at that time is that he would have been entirely unable to conceal the admiration and love he felt for the older man. Rossetti must also have hoped, as I have previously suggested, that this cash-rich undergraduate would be a good source of patronage. But, by 1869 Morris was just as successful as Rossetti if not more so. He was still rich, although the falling value of his invested capital meant that he was increasingly dependent on the profits from Morris and Co. to live as he had done, and he was married to Jane. What was left for Rossetti but to patronise Morris? And what better way to do it than through a little wombat called Top?

Top was for a brief time a member of a household around which pivoted the greatest artists of mid-Victorian England. It would be surprising if he had not played more than a background role as wombats were not common in Victorian London.

This has been a rather sad chapter in what is meant to be a happy book. Contemplating the events of 1869 and 1870 I am filled with sympathy for all of these people who were doomed to be unhappy in their own ways for the rest of their lives. The various twists and turns of their relationships also remind us how dependent on their husbands were Victorian women and how dangerous it was to go down the route of estrangement or divorce, even in socially advanced circles. Jane Morris and Georgiana Burne-Jones were strong and intelligent people but those very qualities must have made it all the more difficult to handle circumstances such as the ones in which they found themselves. William Morris comes across as little less than a saint while Rossetti is like a gifted child. Burne-Jones was left fainting in the street as Luke Ionides led Maria Zambaco home.

To end on a more amusing note here is a poem called *The Last Ditch*. It is taken from E. Nesbit's *Pomander of Verse* (1895) and describes the plight of a woman who has married an artistic man:

> Love, through your varied views on Art
> Untiring have I followed you,
> Content to know I had your heart
> And was your Art-ideal too.
>
> As, dear, I was when first we met,
> ('Twas at the time you worshipped Leighton
> And were attempting to forget
> Your Foster and your Noel Paton).
>
> 'Love rhymes with Art,' said your dear voice,
> And, at my crude uncultured age,
> I could but blushingly rejoice
> That you had passed the Rubens stage.

When Madox Brown and Morris swayed
Your taste, did I not dress and look
Like any Middle Ages maid
In an illuminated book?

I wore strange garments, without shame,
Of formless form and toneless tones,
I might have stepped out of the frame
Of a Rossetti or Burne-Jones.

I stole soft frill from Marcus Stone,
My waist wore Herkomer's disguise,
My slender purse was strained, I own,
But – my silk lay as Sargent's lies.

And when you were abroad – in Prague –
'Mid Cherets I had shone, a star;
Then for your sake I grew as vague
As Mr Whistler's ladies are.

But now at last you sue in vain,
For here a life's commission ends;
Not even for you will I grow plain
As Aubrey Beardsley's 'lady friends.'

Here I renounce your hand – unless
You find your Art-ideal elsewhere;
I *will not* wear the kind of dress
That Laurence Houseman's people wear!

Of course, Jane Morris's espousal of Pre-Raphaelite costume
was so famous (or should that be notorious?) that it was
lampooned in *Punch* as was her general appearance. But I
wonder if her dress and her attempts to take up some of
William's crafts or, indeed, Lizzie Siddal's address to poetry and
painting (much admired by Ruskin of course) was a response
to the dilemma of Nesbit's heroine. It may be the case but, on
the other hand, these were fascinating people who lived in an
edgy relationship with the conventions of their time. But not so
edgy as to break free from them even though they had the
money to do it.

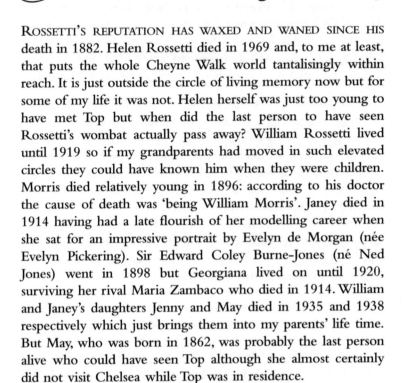

-TOP-
A VALEDICTION

ROSSETTI'S REPUTATION HAS WAXED AND WANED SINCE HIS death in 1882. Helen Rossetti died in 1969 and, to me at least, that puts the whole Cheyne Walk world tantalisingly within reach. It is just outside the circle of living memory now but for some of my life it was not. Helen herself was just too young to have met Top but when did the last person to have seen Rossetti's wombat actually pass away? William Rossetti lived until 1919 so if my grandparents had moved in such elevated circles they could have known him when they were children. Morris died relatively young in 1896: according to his doctor the cause of death was 'being William Morris'. Janey died in 1914 having had a late flourish of her modelling career when she sat for an impressive portrait by Evelyn de Morgan (née Evelyn Pickering). Sir Edward Coley Burne-Jones (né Ned Jones) went in 1898 but Georgiana lived on until 1920, surviving her rival Maria Zambaco who died in 1914. William and Janey's daughters Jenny and May died in 1935 and 1938 respectively which just brings them into my parents' life time. But May, who was born in 1862, was probably the last person alive who could have seen Top although she almost certainly did not visit Chelsea while Top was in residence.

The point is that I have known many people who could have known people who actually saw Top. They could have told me what he looked like. Did he really live, as I think, in a marble kennel after being released from the rabbit hutch in which Harry Dunn had initially penned him? Did he really eat a box of cigars?

There was a flush of interest in Rossetti in the 1930s. John Ferguson and N. C. Hunter had a play called *The Merciless Lady* performed in Birmingham in 1934 and this dealt with the

Lizzie Siddal affair. The next year another play dealing with exactly the same subject appeared in London. This was Herbert de Hamel and R. L. Megroz's *Rossetti*. It was banned following complaints from the Rossetti family but was moderately well reviewed after a private performance. A revival at Chepstow in 1949 was less than successful. The visitations of the Luftwaffe and rationing had obviously made a show about the emotional trials of Victorian artists and the conceit that Lizzie's suicide was effected to enable her spirit to stand between Rossetti and all other women may well have seemed trivial to an audience that had learned that it was possible to destroy whole populations.

But that conceit is, perhaps, not so far from the truth. I am not of course suggesting that Lizzie Siddal killed herself (if she did kill herself) in order to haunt Rossetti. But haunt him she did and the attempt to exorcise that power through exhumation ultimately failed if we are to believe the tales of Rossetti's own fearfulness in the face of his racoon's eerie cries. He had married Lizzie honourably rather than follow his early attraction to Jane Burden and, ultimately, that sense of honour on his part and on Jane's prevented him from rebuilding his life and breaking out of the cycle of addiction and ill health into which he spiralled as the 1870s wore on.

But Top was another brief exorcism. The thought of his plump form gave Rossetti comfort while across London Charles Howell was peering down at Lizzie's reportedly preserved body and while the manuscript book of poems was being disinfected. It was Top who provided a conduit of communication with Jane while she was exiled to Ems. The jokes that Rossetti and his friends played on Morris in their early days together: such as putting a sign reading 'He is mad' on his hat and allowing him to go out with it on, or sewing tucks into his clothes so that the ever portly Morris believed he had suddenly put on weight, must suddenly have seemed less funny when all Rossetti really wanted, whatever he might have admitted to himself, was Morris out of the way.

Top provided a vehicle for that fantasy too. He was, I have suggested previously, a cipher for Rossetti's fantasy of mastering

Morris. But when he died, Rossetti's cartoon of himself weeping over the dead body has a fierce double edge. It is a parody of mourning which, at the same time, rings deeply true. Rossetti buries his face in his pocket-handkerchief over the prostrate body. But the grief is excessive and mocks itself as much through Rossetti's posturing as through the prostrate form of Top and parodic verse that accompanies the drawing. Yet the grief is also sincere as we know that of all Rossetti's beasts it was Top he loved the most. No other creature attracted so many stories and no other still holds our interest as does Top. So when Rossetti chose to call his wombat Top as a way of controlling his rival William Morris he was also, whether he chose to or not, reminding himself of the love he also had for Morris. So Top, harmless and bumbling though he was, offered a focus in Rossetti's home for that lost friendship that he could no longer bear to contemplate, standing as it did between himself and Janey much more effectively than any ghost.

It is also the case that Rossetti's well-padded form mirrors the rotundity of Top. Does Top also stand for Rossetti himself? When we love something I suspect that we all too often love it not only for itself but also for that reflection of ourself we see in it. In drawing himself shedding tears for the death of Top we might also see Rossetti weeping for himself and that lost life that, by 1869, he would have known would never be possible. This is all just fantasy of course but I did promise that we would see Top in every part of his meaning, and the meaning that Top did in some way stand for Rossetti – who was fascinated by the idea of the Doppelgänger (he even figured it in his *How They Met Themselves*) and, as we have seen, seemed to have bilocated himself on occasion – should not be entirely denied. In 1902 Helen Rossetti was having regular visitations from Gabriel during her spiritualist experiments with a planchette but I am pleased to say that the spirit of Top was left in peace.

And there it ends. Top is finally out of reach. Finally beyond our ability fully to understand him no matter how many contexts we try to fit around him. No matter how many ways of seeing him we can devise. Unlike Rossetti or any of the other humans we have met in this book Top didn't keep a diary and there is no collection of his letters. We have to see him through the fragments of other perceptions and to try to piece these together to make some kind of reliable sense. But when it comes to an end, and it *has* come to an end, what Top really means to me now is a fragment of distant life. Something never again retrievable but which is now resilient against all change.

Can we stretch back into a Victorian house and smell it with the keen sense of a wombat? The strangeness of a wombat in Chelsea started me looking for that revival of the past but ultimately Top is no stranger than those who did leave letters and diaries and painting and photographs, and no more or less remote from us.

The painter Dante Gabriel Rossetti had a wombat and called him Top.

A SELECTED BIBLIOGRAPHY

This book is not a scholarly book in the sense that it needs to provide the reader with the kind of apparatus normally found in more serious approach to a topic. It is, however, based on a wide range or primary and secondary sources many of which will enable the interested reader to follow up on some of the hares set running as the story of Top has unfolded.

So here is a list of some of the more interesting and valuable works consulted and not mentioned in the main body of the text:

H. Rossetti Angeli, *Dante Gabriel Rossetti: His Friends and Enemies* (London: Hamish Hamilton, 1949)

H. Rossetti Angeli, *Pre-Raphaelite Twilight* (London: The Richards Press, 1954)

M. Archer, 'Rossetti and the Wombat', *Apollo* (March, 1965)

J. Banham and J. Harris (eds), *William Morris and the Middle Ages* (Manchester: Manchester University Press, 1984)

J. Batchelor, *Lady Trevelyan and the Pre-Raphaelite Brotherhood* (London: Chatto & Windus, 2006)

G. Battiscombe, *Christina Rossetti: A Divided Life* (New York: Holt, Rhinehart and Winston, 1981)

M. Beerbohm, *Rossetti and his Circle* (London: Yale University Press, reprinted 1987)

Q. Bell, *A New and Noble School* (London: Macdonald, 1982)

S. N. P. Benbow, 'Death and Dying at the Zoo', *Journal of Popular Culture*, 37 (2000), pp.379–99

A. R. Bennet, *London and Londoners in the 1850s and 1860s* (London: T. Fisher Unwin, 1924)

A. Bowness et al., *The Pre-Raphaelites* (London: The Tate Gallery, 1984)

A. Briggs, *Victorian Things* (London: Penguin Books, 1990)

M. Bryant, *Casanova's Parrot* (London: Ebury Press, 2002)

J. Bryson (ed.), *Dante Gabriel Rossetti and Jane Morris: Their Correspondence* (Oxford: Clarendon Press, 1976)

J. H. O. Burgess, *The Curious World of Frank Buckland* (London: John Baker, 1967)

P. Burkhardt, 'A Man and his Menagerie', *Natural History* (2001)

H. Caine, *Recollections of Rossetti* (London: Cassell, 1928)

L. Casson, *Libraries in the Ancient World* (New Haven: Yale University Press, 2001)

M. Clark, *History of Australia* (London: Pimlico, 1995)

D. Cowley and B. Hubber, 'Distinct Creation, Early European Images of Australian Animals', *La Trobe Journal*, 66(2000), pp.3–32

A. W. Crosby, *Ecological Imperialism* (Cambridge: Cambridge University Press, 1986)

J. Deordan, *John Ruskin's Dogs* (Bembridge: privately published, 2003)

J. Dimbleby, *A Profound Secret: May Gaskell, her Daughter Amy, and Edward Burne-Jones* (London: Doubleday, 2004)

R. M. W. Dixon, *The Languages of Australia* (Cambridge: Cambridge University Press, 1980)

D. Donald, *Picturing Animals in Britain* (London: Yale University Press, 2007)

R. Dorment, *Alfred Gilbert* (London: Yale University Press, 1985)

R. Dorment et al. (eds), *James McNeill Whistler* (London: Tate Gallery Publications, 1994)

O. Doughty, *A Victorian Romantic* (Oxford: Oxford University Press, 2nd edn, 1960)

O. Doughty et al. (eds), *Letters of Dante Gabriel Rossetti*, 4 volumes (Oxford: Oxford University Press, 1965–7)

H. T. Dunn, *Recollections of Dante Gabriel Rossetti and his Circle* (London: Elkin Matthews, 1904)

D. B. Elliott, *Charles Fairfax Murray* (Lewes: The Book Guild Ltd., 2000)

D. B. Elliott, *A Pre-Raphaelite Marriage* (Woodbridge: Antique Collector's Club, 2006)

J. Evans et al. (eds), *The Diaries of John Ruskin*, 3 volumes (Oxford: Clarendon Press, 1958)

J. R. Feldman, 'Modernism's Victorian bric-à-brac', *Modernism/Modernity*, 8.3 (2001), pp.453–70

H. Finch-Hatton, *Advance Australia* (London: W. H. Allen, 1885)

P. Fitzgerald, *Edward Burne-Jones* (London, Michael Joseph, 1975)

J. Flanders, *A Circle of Sisters* (London: Viking, 2001)

G. H. Fleming, *Rossetti and the Pre-Raphaelite Brotherhood* (London: Hart-Davies, 1967)

J. French, *The Secret World of Wombats* (Sydney: Angus & Robertson, 2005)

R. Gibson, *The Face in the Corner* (London: National Portrait Gallery, 1998)

P. Goldman, *Victorian Illustration* (Aldershot: Scolar Press, 1996)

K. L. Goodwin, 'William Morris' 'New and Lighter Design", *Journal of the William Morris Society*, 2.3 (Winter 1968), pp.24–31

G. Grigson (ed.), *William Allingham's Diary* (Fontwell: The Centaur Press, 1967)

D. Hahn, *The Tower Menagerie* (London: Pocket Books, 2003)

E. Harding (ed.), *Re-framing the Pre-Raphaelites* (Aldershot: Scolar Press, 1996)

T. Hilton, *John Ruskin* (London: Yale University Press, 2002)

B. Jerrold and G. Dore, London: *A Pilgrimage* (London: Grant and Co., 1872)

Jill, Duchess of Hamilton et al., *The Gardens of William Morris* (New York: Stewart, Tabori and Chang, 1998)

Jill, Duchess of Hamilton, *Napoleon, The Empress and the Artists: The Story of Napoleon and Joséphine's Garden at Malmaison* (London: Simon & Schuster, 2000)

K. Kete, *The Beast in the Boudoir* (Berkeley: University of California Press, 1994)

A. Kay, 'The First Bungalow Estate', *Birchington Heritage Trust Newsletter*, November 2002 and February 2003

J. Knight, *The Life of Dante Gabriel Rossetti* (London: Walter Scott, 1887)

L. Lambourne, *Victorian Painting* (London: Phaidon, 1999)

L. Lear, *Beatrix Potter* (London: Allen Lane, 2007)

C. Lloyd (ed.), *The Voyages of Captain James Cook* (London: Cresset, 1949)

P. S. Longhurst, *The Blue Bower* (London: Scala, 2000)

F. MacCarthy, *William Morris* (London: Faber and Faber, 1994)

K. Macdonogh, *Reigning Cats and Dogs* (London: Fourth Estate, 1999)

J. W. Mackail, *The Life of William Morris*, 2 volumes (London: Longmans, Green and Co., 1899)

J. Mackenzie, *The Empire of Nature* (Manchester: Manchester University Press, 1988)

J. Mackenzie, *The Victorian Vision* (London: V&A Publications, 2001)

D. N. Mancoff, *Jane Morris, The Pre-Raphaelite Model of Beauty* (San Francisco: Pomegranate, 2000)

R. Mander, 'Rossetti and the Oxford Murals' in Paris, op. cit.

J. Marsh, *Jane and May Morris* (London: Rivers Oram Press / Pandora List, 1986; revised ed. London: privately published, 2000)

J. Marsh, *Pre-Raphaelite Women* (London: Weidenfeld and Nicolson, 1987)

J. Marsh et al., *Women Artists and the Pre-Raphaelite Movement* (London: Virago, 1989)

J. Marsh, *The Legend of Elizabeth Siddal* (London: Quartet, 1989)

J. Marsh, *Pre-Raphaelite Sisterhood* (London: Quartet, 1992)

J. Marsh, *Dante Gabriel Rossetti Painter and Poet* (London: Weidenfeld and Nicolson, 1999)

J. Marsh (ed.), *Dante Gabriel Rossetti: Collected Writings* (Chicago: New Amsterdam Books, 2000)

G. Meredith, 'A Note on Cheyne Walk', *The English Review*, I (1909), p.333

W. T. Monnington, et al., *Dante Gabriel Rossetti: Painter and Poet* (London: Royal Academy of Arts, 1973)

G. Morey, *The Lincoln Kangaroos* (London: Hodder and Stoughton, 1962)

A. Moyal, *Platypus* (Sydney: Allen and Unwin, 2001)

P. Orpwood, 'The Rossetti Bungalow', *Birchington Heritage Trust Newsletter*, May 2004

L. Paris, *Pre-Raphaelite Papers* (London: Tate Gallery Publications, 1984)

L. Parry (ed.), *William Morris* (London: Philip Wilson, 1996)

C. Patmore, 'Walls and Wall Painting at Oxford', *Saturday Review*, 4.112 (26th December 1857), pp.583–4

C. Payne, *Where the Sea Meets the Land* (Bristol: Sansom and Company, 2007)

G. Pedrick, *No Peacocks Allowed* (Carbondale: S. Illinois University Press, 1970)

L. J. Pigott and L. Jessop, 'The Governor's Wombat: early history of an Australian Marsupial', *Archives of Natural History*, 34 (2007), pp.207–18

E. Prettejohn, *Rossetti and his Circle* (London: Tate Gallery Publishing, 1997)

E. Prettejohn, *The Art of the Pre-Raphaelites* (London: Tate Publishing, 2000)

H. Ritvo, *The Animal Estate* (London: Penguin, 1990)

H. Ritvo, *The Platypus and the Mermaid* (London: Harvard University Press, 1997)

H. Ritvo, 'The Natural World' in Mackenzie ((2001) op. cit.

L. Roberts, *Arthur Hughes His Life and Works* (Woodbridge: Antique Collectors' Club, 1997)

N. Root, 'Victorian England's Hippomania', *Natural History*, 102 (1993), pp.34–39

W. M. Rossetti, (ed.), *Dante Gabriel Rossetti: His Family Letters with a Memoir*, 2 vols., (London: Ellis and Elvey, 1895)

W. M. Rossetti, *Rossetti Papers 1862–70* (London: Sands, 1903)

W. M. Rossetti, *Some Reminiscences* (London: Brown, Langham, 1906)

M. Rothschild, *Walter Rothschild: the Man, the Museum and the Menagerie* (London: The Natural History Museum, 2008)

E. Scigliano, *Love, War and Circuses* (London: Bloomsbury, 2004)

G. R. Sims, *Off the Track in London* (London: Jarrold and Sons, 1911)

Z. Shonfield, *The Precariously Privileged* (Oxford: Oxford University Press, 1987)

D. Stanford (ed.), *Pre-Raphaelite Writing* (London: Dent, 1973)

R. Stott, *Theatres of Glass* (London: Short Books, 2003)

R. Strong et al. (ed.), *A Book of Verse by William Morris* (London: Scolar Press, 1980)

V. Surtees, *The Paintings and Drawings of Dante Gabriel Rossetti (1828–82) A Catalogue Raisonné* (Oxford: Clarendon Press, 1971)

V. Surtees (ed.), *The Diaries of George Price Boyce* (Norwich: Real World, 1981)

D. Sutton, *James McNeill Whistler* (London: Phaidon, 1966)

M. Sweet, *Inventing the Victorians* (London: Faber and Faber, 2001)

A. Thirlwell (ed.), *The Pre-Raphaelites and their World* (London: The Folio Society, 1995)

A. Thirlwell, *William and Lucy, The Other Rossettis* (New Haven: Yale University Press, 2003)

P. Thompson, *The Work of William Morris* (Oxford: Oxford University Press, 3rd edn, 1991)

P. Todd, *The Pre-Raphaelites at Home* (London: Pavilion, 2001)

J. H. Townsend et al., *Pre-Raphaelite Painting Technique* (London: Tate Publishers, 2004)

J. Treuherz et al., *Dante Gabriel Rossetti* (Zwolle: Waanders Publishers, 2003)

B. Triggs, *The Wombat: Common Wombats in Australia* (Sydney: University of New South Wales Press, 1996)

A. Trumble, 'Rossetti's Wombat: A Pre-Raphaelite Obsession in Victorian England' (http://www.nla.gov.au/grants/Harold white/papers/atrumble.html)

A. Vallance, *The Life and Works of William Morris* (London: George Bell and Sons, 1897)

K. S. Walker, *Stunner: The Fall and Rise of Fanny Cornforth* (London: Lulu Publishing, 2006)

D. W. Walton and B. J. Richardson, *The Fauna of Australia*, Volume 1b, *Mammalia* (Canberra: Australian Government Publishing Services, 1989)

F. Watson, *The Year of the Wombat* (London: Gollancz, 1974)

T. Watts-Dunton, 'Rossettiana', *The English Review*, I (1909), pp.323–32

E. Waugh, *Rossetti* (London: Methuen, 1928)

A. L. Webber et al., *Pre-Raphaelite and other Masters* (London: Royal Academy of Arts, 2003)

S. Weintraub, *Four Rossettis* (London: W. H. Allen, 1978)

T. G. Wharton, Martin & Co, *16, Cheyne Walk, Catalogue of the Household and Decorative Furniture* (London: Dandridge, Machine Printer, 1882)

J. Whitehill (ed.), *Letters of Mrs Gaskell and Charles Elliot Norton* (Oxford: Oxford University Press, 1932)

I. Williams, 'Re-Thinking the Legend: Georgiana Burne-Jones and William Morris', *The Review of the Pre-Raphaelite Society*, 4 (1996), pp.1–12

A. Wilton & R. Upstone (eds), *The Age of Rossetti, Burne-Jones and Watts* (London: Tate Gallery Publishing Ltd, 1997)

I. Woodford, *The Secret Life of Wombats* (Melbourne: Text Publishing, 2001)

APPENDIX 1

A Cancelled Entry from *The Dictionary of National Biography*

The following was found among the posthumous papers of Sir Leslie Stephen. It is assumed that Sir Leslie received this as a contribution to *The Dictionary of National Biography* but, for some reason, decided that he would be unable to include it. It is signed 'J. S.' but as the fragment is recovered from a typescript copy of what I assume would have been a manuscript communication I wonder if this should read 'WJS' (for William James Stillman who was both a friend of Rossetti and a prolific contributor to the DNB).

TOP (1867–1869) Wombat. Top was born in Tasmania near the town of Hobart at some time early in 1867. He may well have been in the household of Prince Alfred, Duke of Edinburgh (q.v.) on his ship the *Galatea* when it returned to England in 1868 from the first part of its famous cruise in the southern oceans. Top then lived with Mr Jamrach at his shop on the Ratcliff Highway in London for nearly a year before taking a place in the Cheyne Walk residence of Mr Dante Gabriel Rossetti (q.v.) the celebrated poet and painter in 1869. Top was well known for his charm and for his contributions to the literary and artistic dinners held by Mr Rossetti. He was an acquaintance of Mr James Whistler (q.v.), Mr Algernon Swinburne (q.v.), Mr John Ruskin (q.v.), Mr William Rossetti (q.v.), Miss Christina Rossetti (q.v.), Sir Edward Burne-Jones (q.v.), and many others of the foremost literary and artistic men and women of the time. Top was the subject of a celebratory verse written in Italian by Miss Rossetti and of drawings by Mr Rossetti himself and by his studio assistant Mr Henry Dunn. Top died on 6th November 1869 and although his body was initially preserved by means of taxidermy his resting place is now unknown. J. S.

APPENDIX 2

WOMBAT: A short definition

Waste

Of

Money

Brains

And

Time